THIS BOOK BELONGS TO:

_____

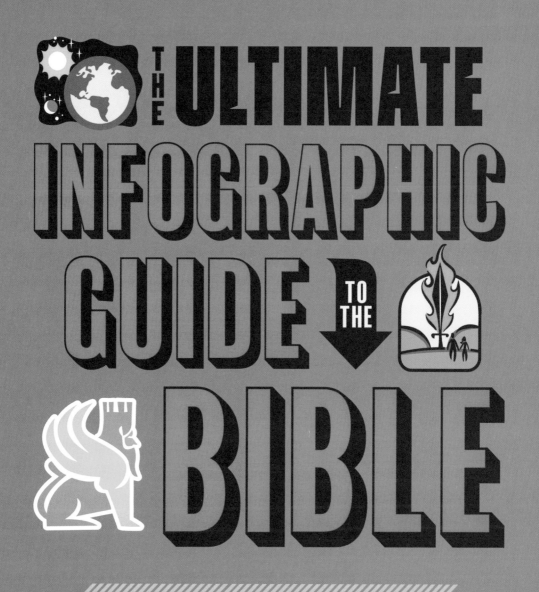

THE ULTIMATE INFOGRAPHIC GUIDE TO THE BIBLE

JOSEPH M. HOLDEN
ILLUSTRATED BY TODD HAMPSON

HARVEST HOUSE PUBLISHERS
EUGENE, OREGON

Cover design by Kyler Dougherty

Cover illustrations by Todd Hampson

Interior design by Janelle Coury

For bulk, special sales, or ministry purchases, please call 1-800-547-8979. Email: Customerservice@hhpbooks.com

Ⓜ is a federally registered trademark of the Hawkins Children's LLC. Harvest House Publishers, Inc., is the exclusive licensee of the trademark.

THE ULTIMATE INFOGRAPHIC GUIDE TO THE BIBLE

Copyright © 2022 — text © Joseph Holden, artwork © Todd Hampson
Published by Harvest House Publishers
Eugene, Oregon 97408
www.harvesthousepublishers.com

ISBN 978-0-7369-8274-0 (hardcover)

Library of Congress Control Number: 2021949964

Printed in China

22 23 24 25 26 27 28 29 30 / RDS / 10 9 8 7 6 5 4 3 2 1

CONTENTS

PART 3: Bible History, the Messiah, and the Future

PART 1

THE STORY
BEHIND THE BIBLE

GENERAL FACTS ABOUT THE BIBLE

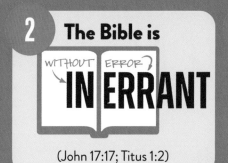

2 The Bible is

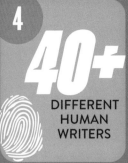

WITHOUT ERROR

IN ERRANT

(John 17:17; Titus 1:2)

3 Written from

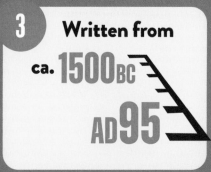

ca. 1500 BC

AD 95

4

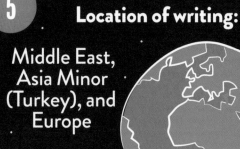

40+ DIFFERENT HUMAN WRITERS

5 Location of writing:

Middle East, Asia Minor (Turkey), and Europe

1 The Bible is inspired by God

Greek: theopneustos

"GOD-BREATHED"

(2 Timothy 3:16; 2 Peter 1:20-21)

6 Earliest book written:

JOB

39 OLD TESTAMENT BOOKS

PENTATEUCH/LAW (5)	HISTORY (12)	POETRY (5)	PROPHETS (17)	
			Major Prophets (5)	*Minor Prophets (12)*
Genesis	Joshua	Job	Isaiah	Hosea
Exodus	Judges	Psalms	Jeremiah	Joel
Leviticus	Ruth	Proverbs	Lamentations	Amos
Numbers	1 Samuel	Ecclesiastes	Ezekiel	Obadiah
Deuteronomy	2 Samuel	Song of Solomon	Daniel	Jonah
	1 Kings			Micah
	2 Kings			Nahum
	1 Chronicles			Habakkuk
	2 Chronicles			Zephaniah
	Ezra			Haggai
	Nehemiah			Zechariah
	Esther			Malachi

7 Latest book written: **REVELATION**

8 **66** books: Genesis to Revelation

9 **929** CHAPTERS in the Old Testament

10 **260** CHAPTERS in the New Testament

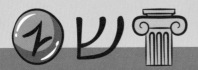

11 **31,100+ VERSES** in the Bible

13 First Bible printed: Latin Vulgate in **1455** by Johannes Gutenberg

12 Original languages of the Bible: Old Testament is Hebrew and Aramaic; New Testament is Greek

27 NEW TESTAMENT BOOKS

GOSPELS (4)	HISTORY (1)	EPISTLES (21)		APOCALYPTIC/PROPHECY (1)
		General (8)	*Pauline (13)*	
Matthew	Acts	Hebrews	Romans	Revelation
Mark		James	1 Corinthians	
Luke		1 Peter	2 Corinthians	
John		2 Peter	Galatians	
		1 John	Ephesians	
		2 John	Philippians	
		3 John	Colossians	
		Jude	1 Thessalonians	
			2 Thessalonians	
			1 Timothy	
			2 Timothy	
			Titus	
			Philemon	

!! THE WORD *TESTAMENT* MEANS **"PROMISE"**

THE INSPIRATION OF THE BIBLE

WHAT IS INSPIRATION?

The supernatural process whereby God "breathes out" the Scriptures (2 Timothy 3:16), who by the Holy Spirit moved upon willing human writers (2 Peter 1:20-21), while at the same time using their unique personalities and writing styles. Since God cannot make mistakes or lie (Titus 1:2), this process guarantees the truthfulness of what is written (John 17:17).

🔑 KEY WORDS

Inspiration (Greek, *theopneustos*) means "breathed out."

Scripture (Greek, *graphe*) means the "writings"—the writings were inspired, not the writers.

🔑 KEY CONCEPTS

- Inspiration means the Bible *is* the WORD OF GOD.
- Inspiration is VERBAL because it was revealed in intelligible words and sentences.
- Inspiration is PLENARY (FULL) because it extends to the whole revelation in all its parts.
- Inspiration implies INERRANCY because God cannot lie, make mistakes, or fail.
- Inspiration gives FINAL AUTHORITY because the words come from God.

🔑 KEY NUMBERS

Though the word *inspiration* (Greek *theopneustos*) is used only once in the New Testament (2 Timothy 3:16), there are more than **2,500** claims to inspiration in the Old Testament Scriptures. These claims are short phrases that attribute words to God, such as "Thus says the LORD..." (Exodus 5:1; Zechariah 8:2).

680 claims in the Pentateuch

418 in the historical books

195 in the poetical books

1,307 in the prophetic books

🔑 KEY PASSAGES

2 Peter 1:21—
The Process of Inspiration

"No prophecy was ever produced by the will of man, but men spoke from God as they were carried along by the Holy Spirit" (ESV).

2 Timothy 3:16-17—
The Source of Inspiration

"All Scripture is given by inspiration of God, and is profitable for doctrine, for reproof, for correction, for instruction in righteousness, that the man of God may be complete, thoroughly equipped for every good work" (NKJV).

🔑 KEY QUESTION

 How can God inspire an infallible book without error through fallible human instruments (writers) who make mistakes?

 God guided the fallible writers through the infallible Holy Spirit to refrain from error when writing the Scriptures (2 Peter 1:21). God drew a perfectly straight line with a crooked stick. Besides, in regular human experience, humans only err sometimes and do not necessarily make errors all the time.

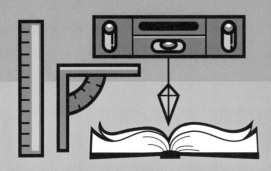

THE CANON OF THE BIBLE

WHAT IS THE CANON?

In classical and biblical usage, the word *canon* means "rule" (cf. Galatians 6:16), "standard," or "measuring rod" (see Ezekiel 40:3; 42:16). Historically, the people of Israel never used the term to refer to their Scriptures. Christians and theologians later used *canon* to refer to the officially recognized collection of inspired books of the Bible.

THREE STEPS OF CANONIZATION

1 *Source:* The inspired books were determined by God.

2 *Discovery:* The people of God recognized which books are inspired.

3 *Collection:* The recognized books were progressively collected and preserved by the people of God into a divinely authoritative canon.

THE FORMATION OF THE OLD TESTAMENT CANON

The Old Testament books, which began to be recorded in the second millennium BC, were written in Hebrew (with some Aramaic). After the books were written, God's people immediately accepted them as Holy Scripture (Daniel 9:2; cf. Jeremiah 25:11). In some cases, they placed these books in the ark of the covenant (Deuteronomy 31:24-26; see also 1 Samuel 10:25; 2 Kings 22:8). The 39 books of the Old Testament were written over a period of ca. 1,100 years (ca. 1500–400 BC). This long period of time is in stark contrast to the New Testament Scriptures, which were written over a span of about 60 years (ca. AD 40–100).

START TO FINISH

A time line of when the church recognized the inspired text and the principles that guided their discovery

1 CA. AD 35–95 The people of God (Christians) immediately accepted the inspired and authoritative books written in the New Testament (2 Peter 3:16; 1 Timothy 5:18). The later acceptance of a canon was for official recognition as the church grew and spread.

2 CA. AD 110 Every book of the New Testament was cited (except two) by Ignatius, Clement of Rome, and Polycarp. By AD 150, the apostolic fathers cited every New Testament book as authoritative.

3 CA. AD 140 The first attempt at a canon was by the heretic Marcion, who rejected the entire Old Testament, apocrypha, and Gospels (except Luke). He accepted the Pauline epistles (except the pastoral epistles).

4 CA. AD 200 L.A. Muratori discovered a canon list in the Milan Library that includes the synoptic Gospels, Pauline epistles, 1 and 2 John, Jude, and Revelation. This is known as the Muratorian Canon.

5 EARLY 4TH CENTURY The Apostolic Canon 85 (final Latin version) accepts all books of the Old and New Testament except Revelation.

6 AD 325 The church historian Eusebius lists all the Gospels, Pauline epistles (except Philemon), 1 Peter, 1 John, and Revelation in the canon. He does not include the general epistles, 2 Peter, 2 and 3 John, and Jude.

7 MID-4TH CENTURY Theodore Mommsen discovered a 10th-century Latin list that contains all but six New Testament books. The list probably originated in North Africa by the 4th century. This is known as the Cheltenham Canon.

8 AD 367 Athanasius, Bishop of Alexandria, lists all 27 books in his paschal letter. This is the earliest complete canon of the New Testament.

9 AD 382/397 The Synod of Rome (382) gave final approval to the canon for all the Western churches. The Synod of Carthage (397) gave final acceptance to the canon to the entire church, thus completing the canon.

THE TRANSMISSION OF THE BIBLE

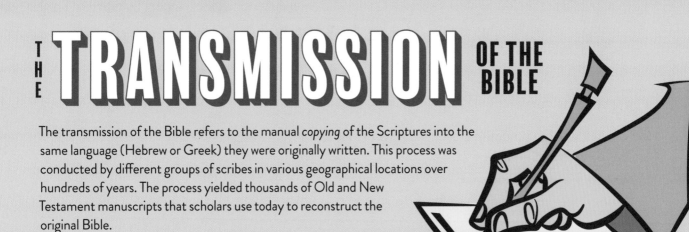

The transmission of the Bible refers to the manual *copying* of the Scriptures into the same language (Hebrew or Greek) they were originally written. This process was conducted by different groups of scribes in various geographical locations over hundreds of years. The process yielded thousands of Old and New Testament manuscripts that scholars use today to reconstruct the original Bible.

ANCIENT MATERIALS OF TRANSMISSION

CLAY
—Artifacts reveal that writing occurred in ancient Sumer by 3500 BC by making impressions with a stylus on moist clay. This method of transmission extended to the biblical prophets to record their books (Jeremiah 17:1; Ezekiel 4:1).

LEATHER
—The more common method of treated animal skin (not pig) was used to ensure longevity and practical transport (Jeremiah 36:23). Durable vellum (calves/antelope, used after 200 BC) or parchment (sheep/goats; 2 Timothy 4:13) were the popular choices for transmitting the Scriptures for over 1,000 years. The *Codex Vaticanus* and *Codex Sinaiticus* are examples of vellum Scriptures (AD 325–350).

WRITING IMPLEMENTS—
Ancient writing implements were available to all the writers of the Bible. These include a stylus for clay and wax tablets, chisel (or iron pen) for writing on stone, and beveled wooden styluses or turkey feathers were used for writing on papyrus and animal skins. The ink was held in an ink horn that the stylus or feather could be dipped into for writing.

STONE
—Portions of the Old Testament Scriptures were chiseled on hard surfaces, such as the law (Deuteronomy 27:2-3; Job 19:24) and the Ten Commandments (Exodus 32:15-16).

PAPYRUS
—Papyrus was an organic plant that flourished in Egypt by 2100 BC. The material from this plant was processed into paper and served as a common writing surface for the early New Testament transmission process (2 John 12; Revelation 5:1). Because papyrus manuscripts are derived from the plant, they are highly perishable. The oldest New Testament fragment (John Rylands Fragment/P52), a portion of the Gospel of John (John 18), is written on papyrus and dates from AD 117–135.

PRINTING PRESS
—By 1455, the Latin Vulgate was printed on paper using a moveable-type press invented by Johannes Gutenberg.

PERIODS OF TRANSMISSION

OLD TESTAMENT

Talmudic Period
(ca. 5th century BC–5th century AD)

- Sopherim (counters/scribes)—5th century BC–3rd century BC
- Zugoth (scribe pairs)—3rd century BC–1st century AD
- Tannaim (teachers)—1st century AD–5th century AD

Masoretic Period
(5th century AD–10th century AD)

- *Masora* means "traditions"
- Extremely careful and reverent copiers
- Added punctuation and vowel points to the text

NEW TESTAMENT

- **AD 100–300:** This period of transmission was characterized by persecution, thus fewer manuscripts come from this era. Scholars rely mostly on lectionaries, inscriptions, short manuscripts, and fragments written in uppercase Greek letters (uncials/majuscules).

- **AD 300–500:** As persecution ends in the early 4th century, an explosion of manuscripts occur that are written mostly on vellum and parchment.

- **AD 60–1000:** As the church expands, Christian monks collected and copied the Scriptures.

- **AD 1000–1400:** As the Word of God spread across the Middle East and Europe, copies multiplied rapidly with a lowercase Greek script (miniscules).

- **AD 1400–1600:** Though handwritten manuscripts continued to be produced during this period, the printing press became the popular mode of producing newly translated works, including the Gutenberg Bible in 1455.

BIBLE = **MOST SUPPORTED ANCIENT BOOK OF ALL TIME**

PRODUCT OF TRANSMISSION

After 3,500 years of scribes and others copying the Scriptures, scholars today have more than 66,000 biblical manuscripts (24,000+ of the New Testament and 42,000+ of the Old Testament) in various forms and languages. The abundance of bibliographical support has established the Bible as the most-supported book from the ancient world, offering readers and scholars confidence that the Bible they are reading today reflects the same Scripture as originally written.

THE TRANSLATION
OF THE BIBLE

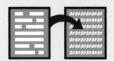

KEY WORDS

TRANSLATION—The rendering of a literary composition from one language to another.

TRANSLITERATION—The rendering of letters from one language into the corresponding letters of another.

Septuagint
Written from 250–100 BC, the Septuagint (LXX) is the Greek translation of the Hebrew Old Testament produced by 70 Jewish scholars in Alexandria, Egypt. This was the most-often used Bible by Jesus and the apostles.

Latin Vulgate
In AD 382, Jerome began translating the Bible into Latin and finished by AD 405. This Bible was adopted by the Roman Catholic Church for the next 1,000 years.

Early Coptic, Latin, Syriac, and Ethiopic
From AD 200–500, early translations in the Egyptian (Coptic), Latin, Syriac (Aramaic *Peshitta*), and Ethiopic languages were completed.

1500 BC

ORIGINAL MANUSCRIPTS
1500 BC TO AD 100

ANCIENT COPIES

ANCIENT VERSIONS
·CODEX ALEXANDRINUS AD 450
·CODEX SINAITICUS AD 400
·CODEX VATICANUS AD 340

LATIN VULGATE
AD 405

MASORETIC TEXTS
135–1200

WYCLIFFE
1382

TYNDALE
1525

COVERDALE
1535

MATTHEWS
1537

GREAT
1539

GENEVA
1560

DEAD SEA SCROLLS (DISCOVERED 1947 AND FOLLOWING)

For centuries, translators have endeavored to make the Bible available in various languages. Through today, Bible translators have rendered the Scriptures in nearly 3,000 different languages.

Wycliffe Bible
Early partial English translations were produced in Britain by Caedmon, Bede, Alfred the Great, and Aldred, John Wycliffe translated the whole Bible from Latin into English by AD 1382.

Tyndale Bible
William Tyndale translated, from the original languages, the complete New Testament in AD 1525 and part of the Old Testament by AD 1535.

King James Bible
At the request of John Reynolds at the Hampton Court Conference in AD 1604, King James I of England enlisted Richard Bancroft to supervise dozens of scholars, divided into teams, to begin a major translation of the Old and New Testaments in English. The project was completed in AD 1611.

TYPES OF TRANSLATIONS

LITERAL TRANSLATION—Word-for-word translation that attempts to stay as close as possible to the biblical text (e.g., NASB).

DYNAMIC EQUIVALENCE—Thought-for-thought translation that modernizes the words and grammar from the biblical text for contemporary readers (e.g., NIV).

FREE TRANSLATION—Paraphrase of sentences and ideas to achieve readability rather than being bound to the original text (e.g., The Message, The Living Bible).

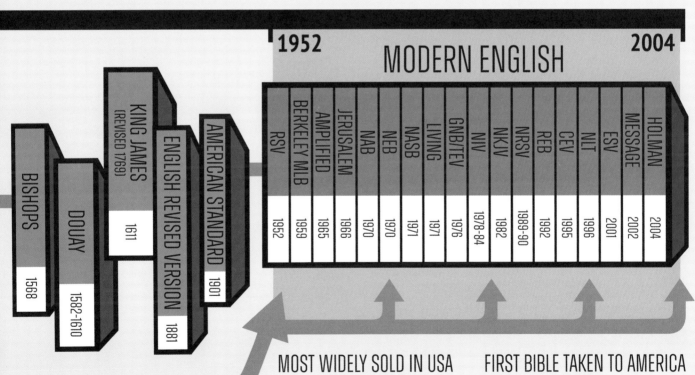

1952 MODERN ENGLISH **2004**

BISHOPS	DOUAY	KING JAMES (REVISED 1769)	ENGLISH REVISED VERSION	AMERICAN STANDARD	RSV	BERKELEY MLB	AMPLIFIED	JERUSALEM	NAB	NEB	NASB	LIVING	GNB/TEV	NIV	NKJV	NRSV	REB	CEV	NLT	ESV	MESSAGE	HOLMAN
1568	1582-1610	1611	1881	1901	1952	1959	1965	1966	1970	1970	1971	1971	1976	1978-84	1982	1989-90	1992	1995	1996	2001	2002	2004

MOST WIDELY SOLD IN USA
NIV, NLT, KJV, ESV, HOLMAN

FIRST BIBLE TAKEN TO AMERICA
GENEVA

FIRST ENGLISH BIBLE PRINTED IN USA
KJV PRINTED BY ROBERT AITKEN, 1782

THE MANUSCRIPTS OF THE BIBLE

Prior to the disappearance of the original Scriptures (*autographs*), handwritten copies (in contrast to *printed* copies) had been made on papyrus, parchment, and leather. These copies are called manuscripts (short for *manual-scripts*) and number in the tens of thousands of copies. The sheer numbers and early dates of these manuscripts give scholars confidence that the Bibles we have today are substantially the same as the original Scriptures.

OLD TESTAMENT MANUSCRIPTS

Prior to 1947, when the Dead Sea Scrolls were discovered, there were relatively few early Old Testament manuscripts. Today, Old Testament manuscripts number in the tens of thousands. Here are a few examples:

Ketef Hinnom Silver Scrolls

In 1980, two small silver scrolls with Hebrew writing were discovered in southern Jerusalem within a tomb complex. These scrolls contained portions of the Old Testament (e.g., Numbers 6:24-26; portions of Deuteronomy, Daniel, Exodus, and Nehemiah). These scrolls are currently the earliest extant Old Testament passages and date to ca. 600 BC.

Dead Sea Scrolls

Every book of the Hebrew Old Testament (except Esther) was discovered in 1947–1956 at Qumran in 11 caves on the shores of the Dead Sea. The earliest of these scrolls date to the 3rd century BC.

Septuagint (LXX)

The LXX is a Greek translation of the Hebrew Old Testament completed in Alexandria, Egypt, during the 3rd–2nd century BC, which became the Bible of Jesus, the apostles, and Greek-speaking Jews throughout the Roman Empire.

Cairo Genezah

In 1890, thousands of Old Testament manuscripts were found in Cairo, Egypt, dating from ca. AD 500–800. Today, these manuscripts are spread around the world in various collections.

Aleppo Codex

Contains the entire Hebrew Old Testament on parchment dating to ca. AD 925.

Codex Leningradensis

Prior to 1947, the Leningradensis was oldest vellum manuscript containing the Old Testament, dated to AD 1008.

NEW TESTAMENT MANUSCRIPTS

There are approximately 26,000–30,000 New Testament manuscripts written in Greek and other languages. They date as far back as the early 2nd century AD and extend to the 16th century AD. The Greek manuscripts alone number 5,860+ copies, which include papyri, lectionaries, and parchment, with the balance comprising manuscripts written in languages other than Greek.

Greek Papyrus Manuscripts

The relatively few but important New Testament papyri manuscripts reflect the earliest copies of the New Testament and date to the 2nd–3rd centuries AD. Among these collections are the Oxyrhynchus Papyri, Bodmer Papyri, and Chester Beatty Papyri, the earliest New Testament scripture being the John Rylands Fragment (P52), which contains a portion of John 18:31-33, 37-38).

Lectionaries

Lectionaries are manuals used throughout the calendar year in church services, and they contain Bible passages written in Greek. There are more than 2,200 of these valuable records, which date from the 4th–12th centuries AD.

Early Church Quotations

The fathers of the early church quoted virtually every book of the New Testament by the end of the 2nd century AD. Today, we can reconstruct the majority of the New Testament with these early quotations of Scripture, which provide a valuable witness to trustworthiness of the text we have today.

Codex Vaticanus

In 1475, the Vatican Library catalogued the Codex Vaticanus (AD 325–350), which contains most of the Old Testament (LXX) and the entire New Testament written in Greek. This valuable manuscript contains the earliest complete New Testament text.

Codex Sinaiticus

Discovered by Constantine von Tischendorf at St. Catherine's Monastery (Egypt) during a series of visits between 1844–1859, the Codex Sinaiticus (AD 350) is a Greek manuscript that contains more than half of the Old Testament (LXX) and all of the New Testament.

TALE OF THE TAPE

MANUSCRIPT COMPARISON
New Testament vs. Ancient Literature

Author	Ancient Title	Date of Original	Earliest Manuscript	Gap from Original	Manuscript Copies
Plato	Dialogues/Tetrologies	4th cent. BC	3rd cent. BC	ca. 150 yrs.	ca. 210–240
Homer	Iliad	9th cent. BC	415–410 BC	ca. 450 yrs.	ca. 1,800+
Herodotus	The Histories	484–425 BC	2nd –1st cent. BC	ca. 450 yrs.	ca. 100+
Thucydides	History of the Peloponnesian Wars	460–400 BC	3rd cent. BC	ca. 200 yrs.	185
Aristophanes	Assorted works	448–385 BC	AD 900	ca. 1,300 yrs.	10
Sophocles	Assorted works	496–406? BC	3rd cent. BC	ca. 200 yrs.	ca. 220+
Julius Caesar	The Gallic Wars	58–44 BC	AD 900	ca. 950 yrs.	ca. 250
Tacitus	Annals of Imperial Rome	AD 58–120	AD 1100	ca. 1,000 yrs.	ca. 33+
Pliny the Elder	Natural History	1st cent. AD	5th & 14th–15th cent. AD	ca. 400–1,500 yrs.	ca. 200
Greek New Testament manuscripts		AD 45–100	AD 117–325	30–300 yrs.	5,860+
Non-Greek New Testament manuscripts (translations)					19,000+
Total New Testament manuscripts					ca. 25,000+

HISTORICAL RELIABILITY OF THE BIBLE

There are three ways historical texts are evaluated for their level of historical reliability:

BIBLIOGRAPHICAL TEST, which examines the quantity, quality, and dating of the biblical manuscripts. This test reveals that there is adequate basis for reconstructing the original biblical text.

- Old and New Testament manuscripts number in the tens of thousands, giving confidence that it is possible to accurately reconstruct the biblical text.
- Every book of the Bible has manuscript support for its reconstruction.
- The New Testament has hundreds of early Scripture notations and announcements (lectionaries) that contribute to the integrity of the biblical text.
- The Bible has the most bibliographical support of any work of ancient literature.
- The early dates of the manuscripts, copied close to the time of the events described in the Bible, do not allow enough time for myth and embellishment to have altered the text.
- Research shows that the accuracy of the transmission of the biblical text stands at more than 99 percent. The small percentage of minor mistakes are due to scribal error (spelling, word order, etc.) and do not affect any major doctrines or historical narratives.

99% ACCURATE
1% MOSTLY ANCIENT TYPOS

MY BAD.

EXTERNAL EVIDENCE TEST

examines the evidence found *outside* the New Testament in disciplines such as historical literature and archaeology.

- There are thousands of artifacts that either directly or indirectly confirm the history recorded in the Bible.
- Archaeological excavation has unearthed dozens of cities mentioned in the Bible that critics formerly claimed were mythological.
- Archaeology has confirmed the past existence of nearly 100 figures mentioned in Scripture.
- Ancient small clay stamp seals (plural, *bullae*; singular, *bulla*) used to seal letters and packages have verified the names and titles of dozens of leaders named in the Bible.
- Ancient coin discoveries have confirmed many rulers, symbols, dates, and religious customs mentioned in the Bible.
- Through inscription discoveries, archaeologists have confirmed the proper ancient titles of rulers and languages spoken throughout the ancient Roman Empire.
- Hundreds of ancient government documents written on clay have confirmed the many events, military exploits, and deeds of rulers and kings mentioned in the Bible (Babylonian Chronicles, Taylor Prism, etc.).
- The James Ossuary (1st-century AD funeral bone box) reflects the earliest witness to the family of Jesus, displaying the Aramaic names of James, Joseph, and Jesus.
- There are more than a dozen pieces of ancient extrabiblical literature, including Jewish literature, that confirm the historicity of Jesus of Nazareth.

INTERNAL EVIDENCE TEST

evaluates the *internal* contents of the biblical writings themselves for evidence of historicity.

- The New Testament retained scenarios where Jesus was cast in a bad or weak light (Acts 10:39). Someone trying to deceitfully support that Jesus was God would not have done this.
- The Gospel writers did not try to harmonize their accounts, which demonstrates they were independent witnesses.
- The writers included difficult passages in the text, something a fraudulent account would not have done (e.g., Jesus said to eat his body and drink his blood).
- They wrote self-incriminating stories without trying to hide the worst situations that occurred among apostles (e.g., Peter's denial of Jesus). Fraudulent authors would not have included these accounts.
- The writers did not deny their testimony under threat of persecution, imprisonment, or death (e.g., Peter and John were arrested and threatened for preaching Jesus in the temple precincts).
- The writers strictly distinguished their own words from Jesus' words, showing they were reporting and not creating fiction (Acts 20:35).
- The first eyewitness reports of the resurrected Jesus came from women, who, in ancient culture, did not have credible legal standing in such matters (e.g., Mary Magdalene).
- The writers said that their records were based on eyewitness testimonies (John 21:24).

HOW WE GOT OUR ENGLISH BIBLE

A Historical Timeline of Translation

1500 BC: God-Inspired Scripture

Though God chose human writers to pen the Scriptures, each of the 39 Old Testament books were inspired (Greek *theopneustos*, "breathed out") by God (1 Timothy 3:16). The Old Testament Scriptures were completed by 400 BC.

AD 40–95: New Testament Written

The 27 books of the New Testament were written by AD 95 in the Koine Greek language.

7th–9th Centuries: Partial English Translations

After the gospel made its way to England by the sixth century AD, partial English translations by Caedmon (Latin to English), Bede (Gospels), and Alfred the Great (10 Commandments/Psalms) were completed.

1537: William Tyndale

The first English translation from the original languages (Hebrew and Greek) was completed in 1530 by William Tyndale (1494–1536). Miles Coverdale helped complete the Old Testament by 1537.

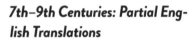

250 BC: Septuagint (LXX)

The first major Bible translation came when the Hebrew Scriptures (Old Testament) were translated into the Greek language for Greek-speaking Jews in Egypt. This is when the titles and divisions of the Old Testament books were first introduced. These same titles and divisions can be seen in today's English Bible.

AD 405: Latin Vulgate

Jerome (Eusebius Heironymous) completed his Latin Vulgate by AD 405, which was a revision of the Old Latin Bible. His Vulgate (meaning "common") was adopted by the Roman Catholic Church and used for the next 1,000 years as their official text. This Bible would later be the basis for the first English Bible.

1382: First English Bible—John Wycliffe

The first complete translation of the English Bible was produced by Oxford scholar John Wycliffe (1329–1384), who translated the Latin Vulgate into English by 1382. By 1388, John Purvey completed a revision that eventually replaced Wycliffe's Bible.

1611: King James Version

The King James Version was commissioned by King James VI after John Reynold's request at the Hampton Court Conference in 1604. Richard Bancroft supervised the translation, which was completed by 1611. The KJV became the most widely read Bible in the 17th and 18th centuries.

PART 2

THE **BOOKS** OF THE **BIBLE**

A BIRD'S-EYE VIEW OF THE WHOLE BIBLE

FOUR SECTIONS OF THE OLD TESTAMENT

The Law (Pentateuch) (1500–1400 BC)

BOOKS: Genesis–Deuteronomy

CONTENTS: Describes creation, the fall, flood, patriarchs, slavery, ten plagues, exodus, Jewish feasts, wanderings, and the tabernacle

CHRISTOCENTRIC THEME: Lays the *foundation* for Christ

Poetry (1500–900 BC)

BOOKS: Job, Psalms, Proverbs, Ecclesiastes, Song of Solomon

CONTENTS: Job's test, David's plea, Solomon's wisdom, life's meaning, and the heart

CHRISTOCENTRIC THEME: Emphasizes the heart's *aspiration* for Christ

History (1400–450 BC)

BOOKS: Joshua, Judges, Ruth, 1 and 2 Samuel, 1 and 2 Kings, 1 and 2 Chronicles, Ezra, Nehemiah, Esther

CONTENTS: Israel's entry into Canaan, the conquest, rise of judges, King David, divided kingdom, fall of Jerusalem, Babylonian captivity, release from Babylon, deliverance of Jews in Persia, rebuilding of Jerusalem and the temple

CHRISTOCENTRIC THEME: Offers *preparation* for Christ

Prophecy (800–400 BC)

BOOKS: Isaiah, Jeremiah, Lamentations, Ezekiel, Daniel, Hosea, Joel, Amos, Obadiah, Jonah, Micah, Nahum, Habakkuk, Zephaniah, Haggai, Zechariah, Malachi

CONTENTS: The major and minor prophets brought messages from God of warning, hope, and future blessing to the people of God

CHRISTOCENTRIC THEME: Describes the *expectation* for Christ

The Bible presents a coordinated and consistent theme of God's redemptive plan for man in eight sections divided equally between the Old and New Testaments. Genesis 3:15 presents the key prophetic and redemptive theme of the Bible, while the remaining books of Scripture present how this promise has and will be fulfilled.

KEY VERSE:

God said to the serpent, "I will put enmity between you and the woman, and between your seed and her seed; he shall bruise you on the head, and you shall bruise him on the heel" (Genesis 3:15 NASB 1995).

FOUR SECTIONS
OF THE NEW TESTAMENT

The Gospels (AD 40–95)

BOOKS: Matthew, Mark, Luke, John
CONTENTS: Presents the biographical portraits of the teachings and acts of Christ as king, servant, man, and the Son of God
CHRISTOCENTRIC THEME: Presents the *manifestation* of Christ

The Acts (AD 60–61)

BOOK: Acts of the Apostles
CONTENTS: Describes the Holy Spirit's activity in the lives of the early believers as they spread the message of Christ throughout the world
CHRISTOCENTRIC THEME: Offers a glimpse of the *propagation* of Christ to the world

The Pauline and General Epistles (AD 50–90)

BOOKS: The Pauline epistles include Romans, 1 and 2 Corinthians, Galatians, Ephesians, Philippians, Colossians, 1 and 2 Thessalonians, 1 and 2 Timothy, Titus, and Philemon; the author of Hebrews is unknown; the general epistles include James, 1 and 2 Peter, 1–3 John, and Jude
CONTENTS: The Pauline epistles give us the doctrinal interpretation of Christ with some application, whereas the general epistles (non-Pauline) offer application with some doctrinal interpretation
CHRISTOCENTRIC THEME: Offers *interpretations* and *applications* of Christ

Revelation (AD 90–97)

BOOK: Revelation
CONTENTS: Provides encouragement and hope to believers in light of persecution and provides insights about the future time of tribulation, with a view toward understanding Christ's second coming to the earth
CHRISTOCENTRIC THEME: Describes the *consummation* of all things in Christ

PANORAMA OF THE OLD TESTAMENT

IN THE BEGINNING...
God creates the heavens, earth, and mankind (Genesis 1)

Adam and Eve sin and are driven out of the garden (Genesis 3)

God promises victory over the devil, though it will cost "the seed of the woman" a great price (Genesis 3)

Noah's ark built and the worldwide flood (Genesis 6–7)

Saul becomes the first king of Israel but disobeys God (1 Samuel 9–10)

The judges rise in Israel to deliver the people from their enemies (Judges)

Joshua and the Hebrews cross the Jordan River and conquer Canaan and settle the land (Joshua 6)

God gives Moses the Ten Commandments, the law, and the feasts (Exodus–Deuteronomy)

The young shepherd David defeats the Philistine giant Goliath in the Valley of Elah (1 Samuel 17)

Samuel anoints David as king of Israel (1 Samuel 16; 2 Samuel 2, 5)

David bears Solomon (2 Samuel 12), who becomes king (1 Kings 1), builds the temple (1 Kings 5–8), and accumulates wealth and wives (1 Kings 10)

After Solomon's death, the kingdom is divided into the northern kingdom of Israel, ruled by Jeroboam, and the southern kingdom of Judah, ruled by Rehoboam (1 Kings 12–14)

The Assyrians destroy Israel (2 Kings 17) but fail to capture the southern kingdom of Judah (2 Chronicles 32)

The books of the Old Testament trace the history of the universe from the act of creation, through the origins of humanity, to a surviving family, through multiplying clans, tribes, and nations, to a focal ancestor, through a chosen tribe and royal lineage, and to the prophets' words of a promised Son who would save the world from its sins.

God causes people to speak in different languages at the Tower of Babel (Genesis 11)

Abraham is called by God to become the father of many nations (Genesis 12)

God destroys Sodom and the cities of the plain (Genesis 19)

Abraham and Sarah bear Isaac, Isaac bears Jacob, Jacob bears 12 sons, and the 12 sons bear 12 tribes (Genesis 21–35)

Moses leads the Hebrews out of Egyptian slavery and journeys to the Promised Land (Exodus 13)

Moses asks Pharaoh to let his people go; Pharaoh refuses, so God smites Egypt with ten plagues (Exodus 7–12)

The Hebrews migrate to Egypt and multiply (Genesis 46–50), then are made slaves by a pharaoh who wasn't familiar with Joseph (Exodus 1)

Joseph's preparations for the famine saves his brothers and the entire region from starvation (Genesis 42–45)

Joseph is betrayed by his brothers, taken to Egypt, sold into slavery, and rises to second in command in the kingdom behind Pharaoh (Genesis 37–41)

King Nebuchadnezzar destroys Judah and Solomon's temple, taking Daniel and his people captive to Babylon for 70 years (2 Kings 25; Jeremiah 25)

The Medes and the Persians conquer Babylon and release the Hebrew captives, though some migrate to Persia (Ezra 2; Daniel 5)

Zerubbabel and Nehemiah leave Persia for Jerusalem to rebuild the temple and the city walls of Jerusalem (Ezra 1–6; Nehemiah 1–3)

The prophets proclaim that the Messiah will come to save Israel and the world from their sins (Isaiah 53; Daniel 9)

GENESIS:

Genesis comes from the Greek translation of the Pentateuch, meaning "origin." The book, written by Moses, records the origins of the world, mankind, sin, the Jewish people, nations, and governments. The creation of the world is described in chapters 1 and 2. Chapter 1 offers a *chronological* sequence of creation in terms of "days" and "evening and morning," and chapter 2 gives a *thematic* review of creation to complete the details. These are one and the same creation account, complementing each other, not two opposing accounts. God did not create out of preexisting matter (*ex-materia*), nor did he create out of himself (*ex-deo*), God created out of nothing (*ex-nihilo*) by giving a verbal command: "God said, 'Let there be light,' and there was light" (Genesis 1:3).

DAYS of CREATION IN THE BEGINNING...

"In the beginning, God created the heavens and the earth. The earth was without form and void, and darkness was over the face of the deep. And the Spirit of God was hovering over the face of the waters" (Genesis 1:1).

 DAY 1: God creates the light (Genesis 1:3)—*to separate day from the night*

 DAY 2: God creates the heavens or sky (verse 6)—*to separate the earth from the sky*

 DAY 3: God creates the seas, plants, and dry land (verse 9)—*to separate the seas from the earth and give us fruits and vegetables to eat*

 DAY 4: God creates the heavenly bodies, sun, moon, and the stars (Genesis 1:14)—*to keep track of times and seasons and to illuminate the night*

 DAY 5: God creates birds and fish (Genesis 1:20)—*to have life in the sky and the seas that would be blessed and multiply*

 DAY 6: God creates land animals and man in his image (Genesis 1:26)—*to have dominion, be fruitful, and populate the earth; to be good stewards and take care of the world*

 DAY 7: God rested from his works of creation (Genesis 2:2)—*to cease from his work of creation, though today he continues to work in and with his creation*

NOAH'S ARK

In Genesis 6, God speaks to Noah and tells him that he is going to destroy the world with a flood because mankind had become irreversibly wicked (verse 13). But God wants Noah and his family (along with pairs of every kind of animal) to survive the flood, so he instructs Noah to build a giant ship, or ark (verse 14). When the ark was finished, it became the most important and unique vessel ever built.

Noah's Family and the Eight Inhabitants of the Ark

- Noah was 600 years old when he entered the ark and lived to 950 years old
- Noah's grandfather was Methuselah (who lived to 969 years old), and his father was Lamech
- Noah was the tenth generation from Adam
- Noah had a wife and three sons: Shem, Ham, and Japheth
- Noah's sons each had a wife
- The inhabitants of the ark were Noah and his wife, Shem, Ham, and Japheth, and their wives
- The eight family members lived on the ark for more than a year and floated on the waters with no means of steering the vessel

Materials and Cargo of the Ark

- Made from gopher wood (like cypress, the same materials used by Phoenicians to build ships)
- The ark was sealed inside and out with pitch, a tarlike substance used to seal joints, seams, and cracks
- The ark was three stories high and had a roof with an opening below it
- Noah spent 100 years building the ark
- For seven days, pairs of clean and unclean animals, both male and female, birds, and every creature that creeped on the ground were brought into the ark
- Then the Lord shut the door of the ark and the floodwaters came

The Ark by the Numbers

The Bible describes the ark measurements in terms of "cubits," which comes from the Latin term *cubitum*, which means "elbow." And though the size of a cubit varied in the Ancient Near East, it is generally considered to be the span between a man's elbow and his fingertips, or about 18 inches (1.5 feet).

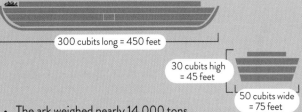

300 cubits long = 450 feet

30 cubits high = 45 feet

50 cubits wide = 75 feet

- The ark weighed nearly 14,000 tons
- The ark was approximately 1,518,750 cubic feet in size (by comparison, the Titanic was three times larger than the ark, with more than 4.5 million cubic feet and measuring 883 feet long)
- The length was equal to one-and-a-half football fields

The dimensions of the ark were perfect for surviving the deluge. The length-to-breadth ratio was 6 to 1, and some modern oil tankers have a ratio of 7 to 1. Interestingly, modern shipbuilders have frequently used the ark's ratio of 30:5:3 up to the 20th century.

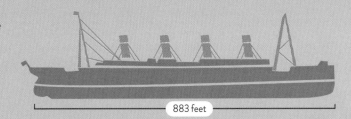

883 feet

The Flood

The "fountains of the great deep burst forth, and the windows of the heavens were opened" (Genesis 7:11).

The rain pours down for 40 days and 40 nights.	The flood-waters continue for another 110 days, at which point the ark stops and rests on the waters.	The waters recede for 73 days before the mountains appear.	Forty days later, Noah opens the hatch and sends a raven and a dove to check for dry land.	Seven days later, the birds return with no sign of dry land. Noah then sends out another dove, and it returns with an olive leaf.	After waiting seven more days, Noah sends out another dove, which does not return.	About three weeks later, the flood ends and the ark comes to rest on the "mountains of Ararat" (Genesis 8:4).	Soon after, God instructs Noah, his family, and the animals to leave the ark.	God makes a covenant promise to Noah and says he will never destroy the earth again with a flood (Genesis 9:8-13). God then confirms the promise with a rainbow.
40	**110**	**73**	**40**	**7**	**7**	**3**		

EXODUS:

KEY MOMENTS IN THE LIFE OF MOSES

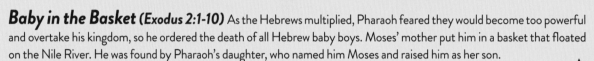

Baby in the Basket (*Exodus 2:1-10*) As the Hebrews multiplied, Pharaoh feared they would become too powerful and overtake his kingdom, so he ordered the death of all Hebrew baby boys. Moses' mother put him in a basket that floated on the Nile River. He was found by Pharaoh's daughter, who named him Moses and raised him as her son.

Killed an Egyptian (*Exodus 2:11-12*) Moses recognized the abuse that his people had to endure as slaves. One day, when he saw an Egyptian beating a Hebrew, Moses killed the Egyptian and buried him in the sand. When Moses' deed was discovered, he had to flee as a fugitive to Midian.

The Burning Bush (*Exodus 2:11–3:22*) While Moses was in exile, God appeared and spoke to him from a burning bush. He instructed Moses to return to Egypt and free his people from slavery. Though Moses did not want to go back, God promised to guide him and said he would send Aaron as well. Moses obeyed the Lord.

The Ten Plagues (*Exodus 7–12*) When Pharaoh wouldn't release the Hebrew slaves, God sent ten severe plagues that devastated Egypt. After the final plague (death of the firstborn), Pharaoh finally relented and allowed the Hebrew slaves to depart for the wilderness to serve God.

Dividing the Red Sea (*Exodus 14*) After Moses and the Hebrews left Egypt with their herds and flocks, Pharaoh changed his mind and pursued them with his army in chariots. As Pharaoh and his army drew closer, the Hebrews were trapped at the edge of the Red Sea. Moses raised his staff and the waters so the people could cross to the other side. Once the Hebrews were safely across, the waters came crashing down on Pharaoh and his army.

The Ten Commandments (*Exodus 19–20*) After the Red Sea crossing, God called Moses to Mount Sinai, where he received the Ten Commandments, which were written on two tablets by God's finger. Moses then delivered the commandments to the people.

The Tabernacle and the Ark
(Exodus 25–28) God gave Moses specific instructions for building a tabernacle and an ark. The tabernacle would be a portable sanctuary where the priests could make offerings to the Lord and God would dwell in the midst of his people. The ark of the covenant, made of wood and overlaid with gold, would hold the Ten Commandments and serve as the place where God would meet the priests.

FAST FACTS ABOUT MOSES

- *Moses* means "out of the water"
- Raised and educated in Egypt by Pharaoh's daughter
- Married to Zipporah
- Had two sons, Gershom and Eliezer
- Had close relationship with God
- Felt he was an inadequate communicator
- Wrote the first five books of the Old Testament
- (Genesis–Deuteronomy), also known as the Torah or Pentateuch
- Known as the lawgiver
- Led his people through the wilderness for 40 years
- Never entered the Promised Land
- Died at 120 years old
- Was buried by God
- Spoke with Jesus in Matthew 17

10 PLAGUES OF EGYPT

While the Hebrews were in slavery in Egypt, God commanded Moses to deliver a message to Pharaoh, saying, "Let my people go, so that they may serve me." Pharaoh refused, And God responded by sending ten devastating plagues, which increased in intensity until Pharaoh released the Hebrews.

PLAGUE 1: *Water Turned to Blood* (Exodus 7:14-25) All the freshwater in Egypt, including the Nile River, was turned to blood for seven days, thus killing the fish and spoiling a necessary commodity for Egyptian life.

PLAGUE 2: *Frogs* (Exodus 7:26–8:15) Aaron stretched his staff over the Nile River and commanded that frogs come forth to cover the entire land of Egypt. The infestation included Egyptian homes and palaces, bowls and cookware. When the plague ended, there were heaps of dead frogs everywhere, causing a foul odor to permeate the land.

PLAGUE 3: *Gnats or Lice* (Exodus 8:16-19) Aaron struck the dust of the earth and it became swarms of gnats (or lice) that covered everything, including people and animals.

PLAGUE 4: *Flies* (Exodus 8:20-24) God caused swarms of flies to invade the land of Egypt, covering the people, their homes, and even the ground on which they walked.

PLAGUE 5: *Death of Egyptian Livestock* (Exodus 9:1-7) God caused a severe plague to come upon the Egyptian livestock in the fields, killing all of them. However, none of the livestock that belonged to the Hebrews died.

PLAGUE 6: *Boils* (Exodus 9:8-12) Because of Pharaoh's continued refusal to release the Hebrews, God brought about painful boils on both people and beasts. The sores affected all living beings; not even wild animals were spared.

PLAGUE 7: *Hail and Fire* (Exodus 9:13-35) Moses brought unprecedented heavy hail mingled with fire on all the land of Egypt, destroying trees, herbs, plants, people, and beasts of the field.

PLAGUE 8: *Locusts* (Exodus 10:12-20) Despite the destruction Egypt endured up to this point, Pharaoh still refused to free the Hebrews. Therefore, God sent locusts to cover the land to the point visibility was impaired and the sky darkened. The locusts stripped bare what little vegetation remained after the hailstorm.

PLAGUE 9: *Darkness* (Exodus 10:21-29) Moses then caused darkness to cover the land for three days. So complete was the darkness that it could be "felt," making it impossible to see anything. But the Hebrews had light in the land of Goshen.

PLAGUE 10: *Death of the Firstborn* (Exodus 12:29-32) After Pharaoh still refused to release the Hebrews, God brought death upon all the firstborn in the entire land, including in the household of Pharaoh. The Hebrews were told they would be spared from this plague if they sacrificed a lamb and applied its blood to the doorposts of their homes. This event marked the first Passover. After this especially painful plague, Pharaoh relented and released the Hebrews from slavery. They went on a journey into the wilderness—a journey called the exodus, which would last for 40 years.

LEVITICUS: THE SEVEN FEASTS OF ISRAEL

During the Israelites' exodus, the Lord instituted seven feasts, or "appointed times," also known as "holy convocations." Each feast corresponded to historical events in Israel's past, or the agricultural cycle, or future events—all of which were part of the Hebrew calendar. The theological and spiritual importance placed upon these feasts served as the calendrical engine that drove the national observance of these appointed times.

TRUMPETS (ROSH HASHANAH) —September/October, Tishri 1
Leviticus 23:23-25

Significance: The Israelites would observe the new year with the new moon with the blowing of trumpets, sacrifices, and a call to repentance before the Lord.

New Testament: For Christians, trumpets foreshadow the new beginning that will be ushered in by the second coming of Christ to the earth.

DAY OF ATONEMENT (YOM KIPPUR) —September/October, Tishri 10 Leviticus 23:26-32

Significance: Once a year, the high priest would offer an animal sacrifice to the Lord to temporarily atone for (cover) the sins of the people. He would sprinkle the animal's blood on the ark of the covenant and release a live goat into the wilderness as a symbol of the release of sins.

New Testament: This day foreshadowed the time when Christ would permanently remove our sin through his death and resurrection from the grave.

PASSOVER —March/April, Nisan 14–15
Exodus 12; Leviticus 23:5

Significance: The people placed lamb's blood on their doorposts in order to be protected from the death of the firstborn (tenth plague). The angel of death, upon seeing the blood, would "pass over" their homes.

New Testament: Jesus (the Lamb of God) fulfilled the Passover through his crucifixion on the cross, and anyone who receives and appropriates his shed blood as payment for their sins will be given eternal life.

UNLEAVENED BREAD —March/April, Nisan 15–22 Leviticus 23:6-8

Significance: The Hebrews quickly prepared to leave Egypt by baking unleavened bread. The time wasted in waiting for the yeast to spread and rise is seen as evil; thus, all leavened foods (symbol of evil) are avoided during this feast.

New Testament: A reminder for us to allow no place for the influence of evil in our lives.

FIRST FRUITS —March/April, Nisan 16 Leviticus 23:9-14

Significance: The Israelites offered to God the first and best of their harvest from the ground as a sign of more plenty to come.

New Testament: Christ's resurrection was the first fruits from the dead, a sign that believers will rise in the future.

PENTECOST —May/June, Sivan 6–7 Leviticus 23:15-22

Significance: The summer wheat harvest was celebrated with the offering of two leavened loaves of bread.

New Testament: Pentecost (meaning "fifty") is the fiftieth day after Christ's crucifixion, the day when the Holy Spirit came upon the church. The leaven refers to the mixed multitude within the church, those who are saved and those who are sinners.

TABERNACLES —September/October, Tishri 15–22 Leviticus 23:33-34

Significance: After leaving Egypt, God provided the Hebrews with food and shelter during their wanderings in the wilderness. This eight-day harvest festival was also called the feast of Booths, or *Sukkot*, because the Israelites built small, makeshift dwellings to commemorate God's provisions.

New Testament: In the millennial kingdom, Christ will provide dwelling places for his people. This feast also signifies the Son of God, or God's provision, becoming flesh and dwelling (or tabernacling) with mankind.

NUMBERS: THE 12 SPIES

Following God's command, when the Israelites arrived at Kadesh-barnea, Moses sent out 12 spies, or one leader from each tribe. These spies were to gather information about the inhabitants and the land of Canaan (Numbers 13:2). This information would help the Israelites to be successful in battle.

THE RECONNAISSANCE MISSION

Moses sent the spies on a 40-day mission to collect the following information (Numbers 13:18-20):

- Were the people who lived there strong or weak, few or many?
- Was the land good or bad?
- Were the cities like camps or strongholds?
- Was the land rich or poor?
- Were there many trees or not?

SPY

THE SPIES & THEIR TRIBES

Shammua (Reuben)
Shaphat (Simeon)
Caleb (Judah)
Igal (Issachar)
Hoshea, or Joshua (Ephraim)
Palti (Benjamin)
Gaddiel (Zebulun)
Gaddi (Manasseh)
Ammiel (Dan)
Sethur (Asher)
Nahbi (Naphtali)
Geuel (Gad)

TRIBE

THE SPIES' REPORT

- The people were many and strong, like giants (Nephilim). In comparison, the spies seemed like grasshoppers.
- The land was good, flowing with milk and honey. The spies brought back grapes, pomegranates, and figs.
- The cities were strong with large walls and fortifications.
- The land was rich in agriculture and architecture.
- The highlands had trees, whereas the coastal plains and the land along the Jordan River did not.

THE RESULT

Ten of the spies brought a bad report and suggested that the people of the land were much too strong to be overcome in battle. However, two of the spies, Caleb and Joshua, believed the Lord would deliver the people and land to them. Tragically, the people of Israel listened to the ten spies who gave a negative report. As punishment for their lack of faith, God said the people and the ten spies would not inherit the land. Only Caleb and Joshua and their descendants would enter the land and possess it because of their faith.

DEUTERONOMY:

THE 10 COMMANDMENTS

While on Mount Sinai in the wilderness, God gave Moses a set of commandments that the Israelites should follow (Exodus 20 and Deuteronomy 5). These were written on stone tablets, and Moses broke the first set of commandments in anger when he found out about the sin that had taken place in the camp while he was up on the mountain (Exodus 32:19; 34:1-4). God gave Moses a second set and promised to bless the Israelites if they faithfully kept the commandments.

DUTIES TO GOD

1. You shall have no other gods before me.
2. You shall not make for yourself any false idols.
3. You shall not take the Lord's name in vain.
4. You shall observe the sabbath and keep it holy.

DUTIES TO MAN

5. You shall honor your father and mother.
6. You shall not murder.
7. You shall not commit adultery.
8. You shall not steal.
9. You shall not bear false witness against your neighbor.
10. You shall not covet.

7 FAST FACTS ABOUT THE TEN COMMANDMENTS

1. Some call the commandments "the Decalogue." In Greek, *deca* means "ten" and *logos* is "word"—thus literally "the ten words," or Decalogue.
2. These commandments are not suggestions or opinions. They are commands, which means we *should* follow them.
3. The Jewish Sabbath starts on Friday night at sundown, whereas for most Christians, the Sabbath is celebrated on Sunday, the day of Christ's resurrection.
4. The commandments were written by the finger of God on stone.
5. The commandments were placed inside the ark of the covenant.
6. The last six commandments regarding the duties to man have been universally incorporated into the moral codes and laws of many countries, while governments allow varying amounts of freedom or restrictions in relation to exercising the first four commands.
7. The commandments are not meant to unnecessarily restrict our lives, but to enhance our lives and make them more enjoyable.

2 POSSIBLE ROUTES

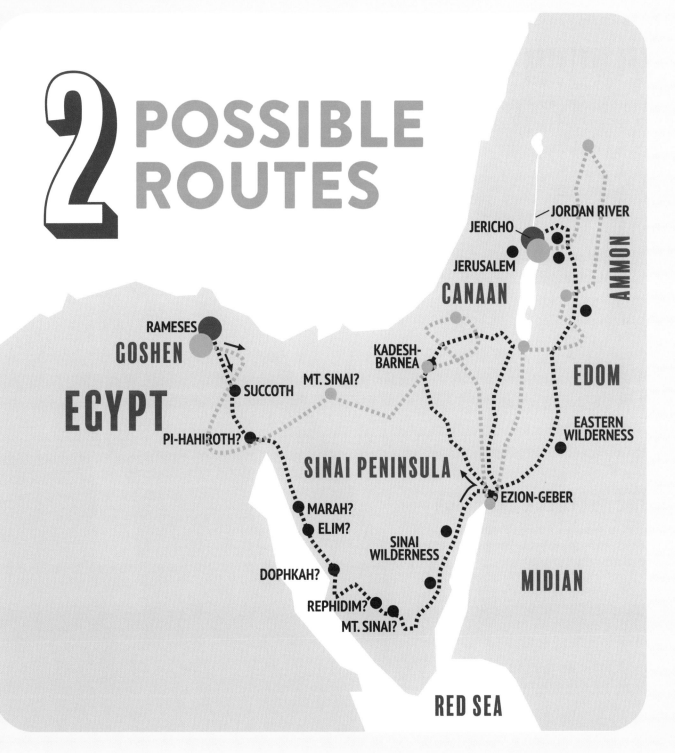

JOSHUA: THE CONQUEST OF CANAAN

After the death of Moses, God called Joshua to conquer the Promised Land (Joshua 2–11). This tall order was compounded by the fact the people who lived in that land had sophisticated fortifications and weapons, high-walled cities, large numbers of combatants, and great physical stature. The Israelites were up against great odds, which required them to put their faith in God's promise to lead and protect them in battle.

THE SOUTHERN CAMPAIGN

After the Israelites left their camp at Abel Shittim and crossed the Jordan River, they camped at Gilgal. From there, they began by attacking the walled city of Jericho.

1. Depart from Abel Shittim (Joshua 3:1)
2. Camp at Gilgal (4:19)
3. Jericho (6:1-27)
4. Ai (8:1-29)
5. Ammorites in the Valley of Ajalon (9:1–10:14)
6. Gibeon (10:6-15)
7. Beth Horon (10:6-15)
8. Makkedah, Libnah (10:16-30)
9. Gezer (10:16-30)
10. Lachish (10:33)
11. Eglon (10:34-35)
12. Hebron (10:36-37)
13. Debir (10:38-39)
14. Kadesh-Barnea (10:41)
15. Gaza (10:41)

THE NORTHERN CAMPAIGN

After conquering southern Canaan, Joshua and his army returned to Gilgal before they turned their attention to northern Canaan.

16. The confederacy at the waters of Merom (near Kedesh) (11:1-8)
17. Sidon (11:8)
18. Misrephoth-Maim (11:8)
19. Valley of Mizpah (11:8)
20. Hazor (11:10-15)

After the campaigns were finished, Joshua defeated the Anakim (giants) from the hill country and from Hebron, Debir, and Anab. Only a few remained in the Philistine cities of Gaza, Ashdod, and Gath, of which Goliath was one. "So Joshua took the whole land, according to all that the LORD had spoken to Moses" (Joshua 11:23).

LAND FOR THE 12 TRIBES OF ISRAEL

After the Israelite conquest of the Promised Land, Joshua set aside portions of land for each of the 12 tribes as an inheritance (Joshua 11:23). The allotments were as follows:

ASHER

NAPHTALI

ZEBULUN

ISSACHAR

← MANASSEH →

DAN

EPHRAIM

GAD

BENJAMIN

REUBEN

JUDAH

SIMEON

JUDGES: THE JUDGES OF ISRAEL

The book of Judges takes its name from the 12 civil and military rulers, or judges, who delivered Israel from multiple cycles of oppression over a period of about 400 years. During this time of national decline and chaos, "there was no king in Israel" and "everyone did what was right in their own eyes" (Judges 21:25). The events described in Judges 2–16 took place between Joshua's death (14th century BC) and the rise of the prophet Samuel (11th century BC) and are a testimony to God's preservation of Israel.

1. **OTHNIEL** (3:7-11) From the tribe of Judah, Othniel gave Israel 40 years of peace after he delivered the nation from the oppressive Mesopotamian king Cushan-Rishathaim.

2. **EHUD** (3:12-30) From the tribe of Benjamin, the left-handed Ehud killed the Moabite king Eglon, who sought to rule Israel harshly. The resulting peace lasted for 80 years.

3. **SHAMGAR** (3:31) Shamgar battled the Philistine oppressors, saving Israel using an oxgoad (a long sharp stick) to kill 600 Philistine warriors.

4. **DEBORAH** (4–5) From the Tribe of Ephraim, Deborah was the only female judge. She fought against King Jabin of the Canaanites as well as his most formidable general, Sisera, defeating them soundly and giving Israel a peace that lasted for 40 years.

5. **GIDEON** (6–8) From the tribe of Manasseh, Gideon delivered the Israelites from Midianite oppression. In a surprise nighttime attack with only 300 men, he destroyed the Midianite camp, bringing peace to Israel for 40 years.

6. **TOLA** (10:1-2) From the tribe of Issachar, not much information is provided about Tola except that he was the son of Puah and lived in the hill country of Ephraim. He reigned for 23 years.

7. **JAIR** (10:3-5) As a Gileadite most likely from the tribe of Manasseh, Jair had 30 sons who rode 30 donkeys, and he ruled 30 cities called Havvoth Jair. He judged for 22 years, then was buried in Kamon.

8. **JEPHTHAH** (10:6–12:7) Jephthah was a Gileadite who, early on, was banished from his home because he was the son of a prostitute. Later, the people of Israel would call upon him to deliver them from the Ammonites (descendants of Lot), who sought to make war and oppress the Israelites. He ruled for six years and brought peace to Israel for 24 years.

9. **IBZAN** (12:8-10) From Bethlehem, Ibzan had 30 sons and 30 daughters. He ruled Israel for seven years and brought seven years of peace to Israel.

10. **ELON** (12:11-12) From the tribe of Zebulun, Elon judged for ten years, bringing ten years of peace to Israel. After his death he was buried in Aijalon, in the land of Zebulun.

11. **ABDON** (12:13-15) From the tribe of Ephraim, Abdon had 40 sons and 30 grandsons who rode on 70 donkeys. He ruled for eight years and brought peace to Israel during his tenure. He was buried in Pirathon in the land of Ephraim, in the hill country of the Amalekites.

12. **SAMSON** (13-16) From the tribe of Dan, Samson was a Nazirite who was to abstain from cutting his hair and from drinking alcohol. God gave Samson supernatural strength, which he used to deliver Israel from the Philistines. Among his feats were killing a lion and striking down 1,000 Philistines with a donkey's jawbone. He judged Israel for 20 years. He fell in love with a Philistine woman named Delilah, who discovered the source of his strength and betrayed him to his enemies. After being taken captive, he died—and killed 3,000 of his enemies along with him—when he destroyed a Philistine temple by pushing out the foundational pillars.

RUTH: THE STORY OF RUTH

Ruth and Esther are the only two books of the Bible named after women. Ruth offers a lovely story of God at work to create beauty from ashes. A Moabite woman, Ruth entered the genealogy of Jesus through her marriage to a Davidic patriarch, the wealthy landowner named Boaz, the grandfather of King David.

TIMELINE

Ruth 1
- Naomi and her husband, Elimelech, who were Israelites, journey to Moab with their sons, Mahlon and Chilion, to avoid the famine in Bethlehem.
- Naomi's sons marry Moabite women, Orpah and Ruth.
- Naomi's entire family dies, leaving only Orpah and Ruth.
- Ruth bonds with Naomi, making Naomi's people her people and Naomi's God her God.
- Naomi and Ruth return to Bethlehem.

Ruth 2
- Ruth gleans in Boaz's field.
- Ruth meets Boaz, a wealthy landowner.

Ruth 3
- At Boaz's threshing floor, Ruth asks Boaz to marry her.

Ruth 4
- Ruth and Boaz marry.
- Ruth gives birth to Obed.
- Naomi receives a new family.

Adam
Noah
Shem
Abraham
Isaac
Jacob
Judah
Perez
Hezron
Ram
Amminidab
Nahshon
Salmon
Boaz & Ruth
Obed
Jesse
David

JESUS

GENEALOGY

Ruth wasn't the only foreign woman in the genealogy of Jesus; Tamar and Rahab were also foreign women. The following genealogy lists the lineage that was "fathered," which can mean "fathered an ancestor," meaning that there could be ancestral gaps in the genealogy (Ruth 4:18-20).

1 SAMUEL: DAVID AND GOLIATH

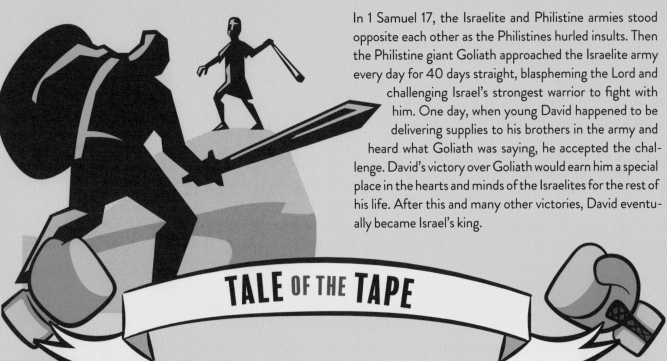

In 1 Samuel 17, the Israelite and Philistine armies stood opposite each other as the Philistines hurled insults. Then the Philistine giant Goliath approached the Israelite army every day for 40 days straight, blaspheming the Lord and challenging Israel's strongest warrior to fight with him. One day, when young David happened to be delivering supplies to his brothers in the army and heard what Goliath was saying, he accepted the challenge. David's victory over Goliath would earn him a special place in the hearts and minds of the Israelites for the rest of his life. After this and many other victories, David eventually became Israel's king.

TALE OF THE TAPE

	DAVID	VS.	GOLIATH
Location	Valley of Elah		Valley of Elah
Country	Israelite of Bethlehem		Philistine of Gath
Family	Youngest of 8 sons of Jesse		Had brothers
Occupation	Shepherd		Champion warrior
Age	Handsome youth		Giant adult
Height	Much smaller than Goliath		6 cubits+ span (9 feet 6 inches)
Experience	Killed a bear and a lion		Battle-hardened warrior
Attitude/Mindset	Humble confidence with faith		Overconfident without faith
Occasion	Delivering 10 loaves of bread, 10 wheels of cheese, and dried grain to his older brothers in the army		Came to fight and kill Israelite soldiers, blaspheme God, and challenge the strongest Israelite soldier to a match
Reason for Fighting	Honor God		Enslave Israel
Armor	God		A guard, body shield, bronze helmet, bronze leg guards, bronze chest plate, and a coat of mail that weighed 125–155 pounds
Weapons	Shepherd's staff, 5 smooth stones, and a slingshot		A sword and a large spear with a shaft the size of a weaver's beam, with an iron tip that weighed 15–19 pounds
Result	God was vindicated, David gained favor, took Goliath's head and armor to his tent, Israelite army victorious		Philistine gods were diminished, Goliath was dead, Philistine army retreated in defeat

2 SAMUEL: LIFE AND TIMES OF KING DAVID

King David flourished ca. 1011–971 BC until his son, Solomon, became king ca. 971 BC. Under David's reign, the Israelite kingdom became firmly established and many military battles were won. Despite David's failures, God made him the preeminent king in all the earth and his descendants would not only sit on the throne after him, but become the lineage through which the promised Messiah, Jesus, would be born (2 Samuel 7; Psalm 89:3-4).

WIVES AND SONS OF DAVID

WIVES		SONS
Ahinoam	⟶	Amnon
Abigail	⟶	Chileab
Maacha	⟶	Absalom
Haggith	⟶	Adonijah
Abital	⟶	Shephatiah
Eglah	⟶	Ithream
Bathsheba	⟶	Solomon, Shimea, Shobab, and Nathan
Michal	⟶	None
Concubines	⟶	Ibhar, Elishama, Eliphelet, Nogah, Nepheg, Japhia, Eliada

DAVID'S LIFE AND CAREER

- David was the youngest of the eight sons of Jesse (son of Ruth) and lived in Bethlehem.
- David was a ruddy young shepherd, a man after God's own heart, who defeated a lion and a bear who attacked his sheep (1 Samuel 13:13-14; 1 Samuel 17).
- The prophet Samuel anointed David as the future king of Israel while King Saul was still on the throne (1 Samuel 16).
- David defeated Goliath in battle and gained favor as the king's musician and armor bearer (1 Samuel 16:22-23).
- King Saul became jealous and persecuted David, causing him to flee for his life.
- At 30 years old, David became king after Saul killed himself in battle (1 Samuel 31:4; 2 Samuel 2, 5).
- David and his army captured the Jebusite stronghold at Jerusalem, which then became the city of David (2 Samuel 5:4-13; 1 Chronicles 21). Jerusalem was made the capital of David's kingdom.
- King Hiram of Tyre sent skilled workers and building materials to David so David could build a palace for himself (2 Samuel 5:11).
- David brought the ark of the covenant to Jerusalem (2 Samuel 6).
- Though David could not build a dwelling place for God, God made a covenant with David and promised a dynasty that would descend from his son Solomon—a dynasty that would last forever, known as the House of David (2 Samuel 7).
- David committed adultery with Bathsheba and had her husband, Uriah, killed in battle. For this sin, God took the life of David and Bathsheba's first child (2 Samuel 11–12).
- David and Bathsheba gave birth to Solomon, who would later become David's successor.
- David purchased the threshing floor of Araunah, which would later become the site where Solomon would build the first temple (2 Samuel 24).
- David reigned in Hebron for seven years and Jerusalem for 33 years (2 Samuel 5:3-5), ruling over Israel for a total of 40 years (1 Kings 2:11).
- David anointed Solomon as king (1 Kings 1).
- Upon his death, David was buried in the city of David (1 Kings 2:10).

1 KINGS: THE KINGDOM IS DIVIDED

Because Solomon did not follow God's instructions, God said he would tear the kingdom from his family (1 Kings 11:11). After he died, the kingdom was divided. Solomon's son, Rehoboam, reigned in the south over the tribes of Judah and Benjamin (Judah), while Jeroboam ruled the north over the other ten tribes (Israel). All the kings of Israel disobeyed the Lord, while the kings of Judah were mostly evil with a few good ones every now and then. The northern kingdom of Israel was conquered and taken captive by the Assyrians in ca. 722 BC, and the southern kingdom Judah was destroyed by the Babylonians in ca. 586 BC.

UNITED KINGDOM

UNITED MONARCHY (ISRAEL)

Saul	1051–1011 BC
David	1011–971
Solomon	971–931

DIVIDED KINGDOM

SOUTHERN KINGDOM OF JUDAH

Rehoboam	931–913 BC
Abijah	931–911
Asa	911–870
Jehoshaphat	872–848
Jehoram	853–841
Ahaziah	841
Athaliah	841–835
Joash (Jehoash)	835–796
Amaziah	796–792
Azariah (Uzziah)	792–740
Jotham	750–732
Ahaz	735–716
Hezekiah	716–687
Manasseh	697–643
Amon	643–641
Josiah	641–609
Jehoahaz	609
Jehoiakim	609–598
Zedekiah	597–586

NORTHERN KINGDOM OF ISRAEL

Jeroboam	931–910 BC
Nadab	910–909
Baasha	909–886
Elah	886–885
Zimri	885
Omri	885–874
Ahab	874–853
Ahaziah	853–852
Jehoram (Joram)	852–841
Jehu	841–814
Jehoahaz	814–798
Jeroboam II	793–753
Zachariah	753–752
Shallum	752
Menahem	752–742
Pekahiah	742–740
Pekah	752–732
Hoshea	732–722

2 KINGS: THE MIRACLES OF ELIJAH AND ELISHA

In 1 and 2 Kings we read about Elijah and his disciple Elisha, who were prophets of God and were empowered to perform miracles. Seven miracles are associated with Elijah, and 15 with Elisha.

MIRACLES OF ELIJAH

1. **Elijah is fed by ravens** (1 Kings 17:6).

2. **Elijah creates food for the widow** (1 Kings 17:14).

3. **Elijah raises a dead boy to life** (1 Kings 17:22).

4. **Elijah defeats the prophets of Baal with fire from heaven** (1 Kings 18:38).

5. **Elijah brings down fire from the sky to consume fifty soldiers** (2 Kings 1:10).

6. **Elijah divides the Jordan River** (2 Kings 2:8).

7. **Elijah is taken to heaven in a fiery chariot by a whirlwind** (2 Kings 2:11).

MIRACLES OF ELISHA

1. **Elisha divides the Jordan River** (2 Kings 2:14).

2. **Elisha makes poisoned waters fresh** (2 Kings 2:21).

3. **Elisha curses a group of bullies, of which 42 were mauled by two bears** (2 Kings 2:24).

4. **Elisha fills empty containers with oil for a widow** (2 Kings 4:3).

5. **Elisha prophesies a child would be born** (2 Kings 4:17).

6. **Elisha brings the Shunammite's son back to life** (2 Kings 4:35).

7. **Elisha makes poisonous food safe** (2 Kings 4:41).

8. **Elisha multiplies loaves** (2 Kings 4:43-44).

9. **Elisha heals Naaman of leprosy** (2 Kings 5:14).

10. **Elisha makes iron (axe head) to float** (2 Kings 6:6).

11. **Elisha gives spiritual sight** (2 Kings 6:17).

12. **Elisha strikes the Syrian soldiers with blindness** (2 Kings 6:18).

13. **Elisha gives sight to the Syrian soldiers** (2 Kings 6:20).

14. **Elisha prophesies the availability of food** (2 Kings 7:1).

15. **Elisha brings a Moabite man to life** (2 Kings 13:21).

1 CHRONICLES:
TIMELINE OF DAVID'S LIFE AND REIGN

the ups... and downs... of David's life.

- Birth 1041 BC (2 Samuel 5:4-5)
- Anointed by Samuel 1029 (1 Samuel 16:1-13)
- Slays Goliath the Philistine at the Valley of Elah 1024 (1 Samuel 17)
- Flees from Saul 1020–1011 (1 Samuel 21–31)
- Saul dies (1 Samuel 31:4-5)
- Anointed as king of Judah 1011 (2 Samuel 2:1-4)
- Reigns from Hebron for 7.5 years (2 Samuel 5:5)
- Becomes king over Israel 1004
- Battles the Philistines 1004 (2 Samuel 5:17-25)
- Defeats the Jebusites and takes Jerusalem 1004 (2 Samuel 5:6-10)
- Three years of famine 996–993 (2 Samuel 21:1-14)
- Battles the Ammonites 993–990 (2 Samuel 10–12)
- David and Bathsheba commit adultery 992 (2 Samuel 11)
- Murder of Uriah (Bathsheba's husband) 992 (2 Samuel 11)
- Death of David and Bathsheba's firstborn child 992 (2 Samuel 12:15-23)
- Rape of Tamar 987 (2 Samuel 13:1-22)
- Death of Amnon 985 (2 Samuel 13:23-26)

- Absalom goes into exile 985–982 (2 Samuel 13:37-39)
- Absalom returns to Jerusalem 982–980 (2 Samuel 14:21-24)
- Builds the royal palace in the city of David 980–978 (1 Chronicles 15:1)
- Builds the tabernacle in Jerusalem 977 (1 Chronicles 15:1)
- Brings the ark of the covenant to Jerusalem 977 (2 Samuel 14:21-24)
- Absalom rebels 976 (2 Samuel 15–18)
- David goes into exile 976 (2 Samuel 15–18)
- Conducts a census, and God punishes him 975 (2 Samuel 24:1-17)
- Purchases the threshing floor of Aruanah (temple site) 973 (2 Samuel 24:18-25)
- God makes a covenant with David 973 (2 Samuel 7)
- Solomon becomes coregent 973–971 (1 Chronicles 23:1)
- Adonijah attempts to become king 972 (1 Kings 1:5-37)
- Solomon expels Adonijah and becomes king 971 (1 Chronicles 29:22-23)
- David dies 971 (1 Kings 2:10-11)

2 CHRONICLES:
CHARACTERISTICS OF SOLOMON'S TEMPLE

Solomon, the son of King David, built the temple to replace the tabernacle (2 Chronicles 2–7). His chosen site was in Jerusalem on Mount Moriah (2 Chronicles 3:1). After this temple was destroyed by the Babylonians in 586 BC (2 Kings 25:8-9), two additional temples were built at the same location: one by Zerubbabel (ca. 515 BC), and the other by King Herod (ca. 20 BC). Herod's temple was destroyed by the Romans in AD 70.

The Bible describes for us these characteristics about Solomon's temple:

START DATE: ca. 967 BC (1 Kings 6:1; 2 Chronicles 3:1-2)

DATE OF DEDICATION: ca. 960–959 (1 Kings 6:38)

DIMENSIONS: The temple was 90 feet long, 30 feet wide, and 45 feet high (1 Kings 6:1-10).

STRUCTURE: The temple was a three-chambered (tripartite) building consisting of the Holy of Holies, the Holy Place, and the porch, which was surrounded by a courtyard platform supported by retaining walls.

MATERIALS: The temple was made of quarried limestone covered with panels of cedar and overlaid in places with gold (2 Kings 6).

ENTRY COURTYARD: In the courtyard was the altar for sacrifices (2 Chronicles 4:1) and the laver (*yam*) filled with 12,000 gallons of water, which set upon 12 bronze oxen and was used for priestly ritual cleansing (1 Kings 7:23-26; 2 Chronicles 4:2-5). There were other smaller bronze laver carts (*mechonot*) with wheels situated on each side of the courtyard for the washing of animals (1 Kings 7:27-38).

PILLARS: At the front of the temple, on each side of the porch entrance, were two hollow bronze pillars named Boaz and Jachin (1 Kings 7:21; 2 Chronicles 3:17).

DOORS: Two gold-overlaid folding doors led from the porch or vestibule to an interior nave or the Holy Place (1 Kings 6:33-35).

HOLY PLACE: In the Holy Place was the golden altar of incense and the golden table for the bread of presence, along with ten golden lampstands—five on the north side and five on the south (1 Kings 7:48-49).

HOLY OF HOLIES: Inside the Holy of Holies stood two massive 15-foot-tall golden cherubim on the ark of the covenant, which was made of wood overlaid with gold (1 Kings 6:23-28; 2 Chronicles 5:1-14).

EZRA: THE EXILES RETURN TO JERUSALEM

The book of Ezra describes the restoration of Israel after 70 years of Babylonian captivity comes to an end in 536 BC (Jeremiah 25:11-12). King Cyrus of Persia proclaimed that the Jewish exiles could return home and build their city and religious temple (Ezra 1:1-4). The people's return to Jerusalem would occur over the course of three journeys led by different people. Two of these journeys are recorded in the book of Ezra, and the third journey is described in the book of Nehemiah. The map illustrates the routes of the three journeys to Jerusalem.

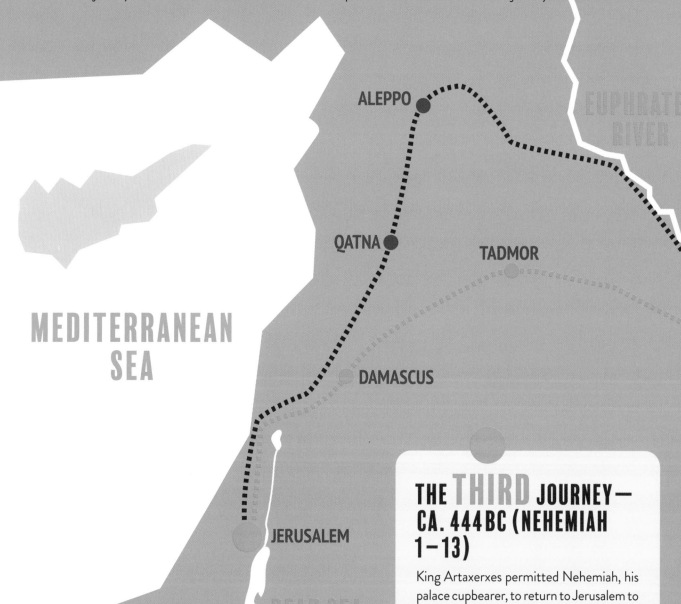

ALEPPO

EUPHRATES RIVER

QATNA

TADMOR

MEDITERRANEAN SEA

DAMASCUS

JERUSALEM

DEAD SEA

THE THIRD JOURNEY— CA. 444 BC (NEHEMIAH 1–13)

King Artaxerxes permitted Nehemiah, his palace cupbearer, to return to Jerusalem to rebuild the broken-down walls and dilapidated infrastructure (Nehemiah 1–2). This group left from Shushan (Susa) in Persia with an unknown number of people and had to travel a much longer distance than the first two groups.

THE FIRST JOURNEY—CA. 536 BC (EZRA 1–6)

The first group of about 50,000 exiles was led by Zerubbabel (Ezra 2:1-2), also known to the Persians as Sheshbazzar (Ezra 1:11; 2:2; 5:14; cf. Haggai 1:14). The long journey of 500 miles would have taken four months to complete. This is why some of the people did not return to Jerusalem when they had the chance to do so. Those who made the trip started the work of rebuilding the temple (Ezra 3:8), but then the construction activity stopped for many years. Not until 20 years later, in 516 BC, was the temple finally completed (Ezra 4:24; 6:15).

THE SECOND JOURNEY— CA. 457 BC (EZRA 7–10)

Between the first and second journeys, the events of the book of Esther took place in Shushan (Persia). Nearly 80 years would pass before the second group left from Babylon. About 457 BC, during the reign of King Artaxerxes of Persia, Ezra the scribe led the second wave of exiles, about 1,500 of them, on the four-month journey back to Jerusalem. When he arrived, he turned his attention to rebuilding the nation's spiritual health (Ezra 9–10).

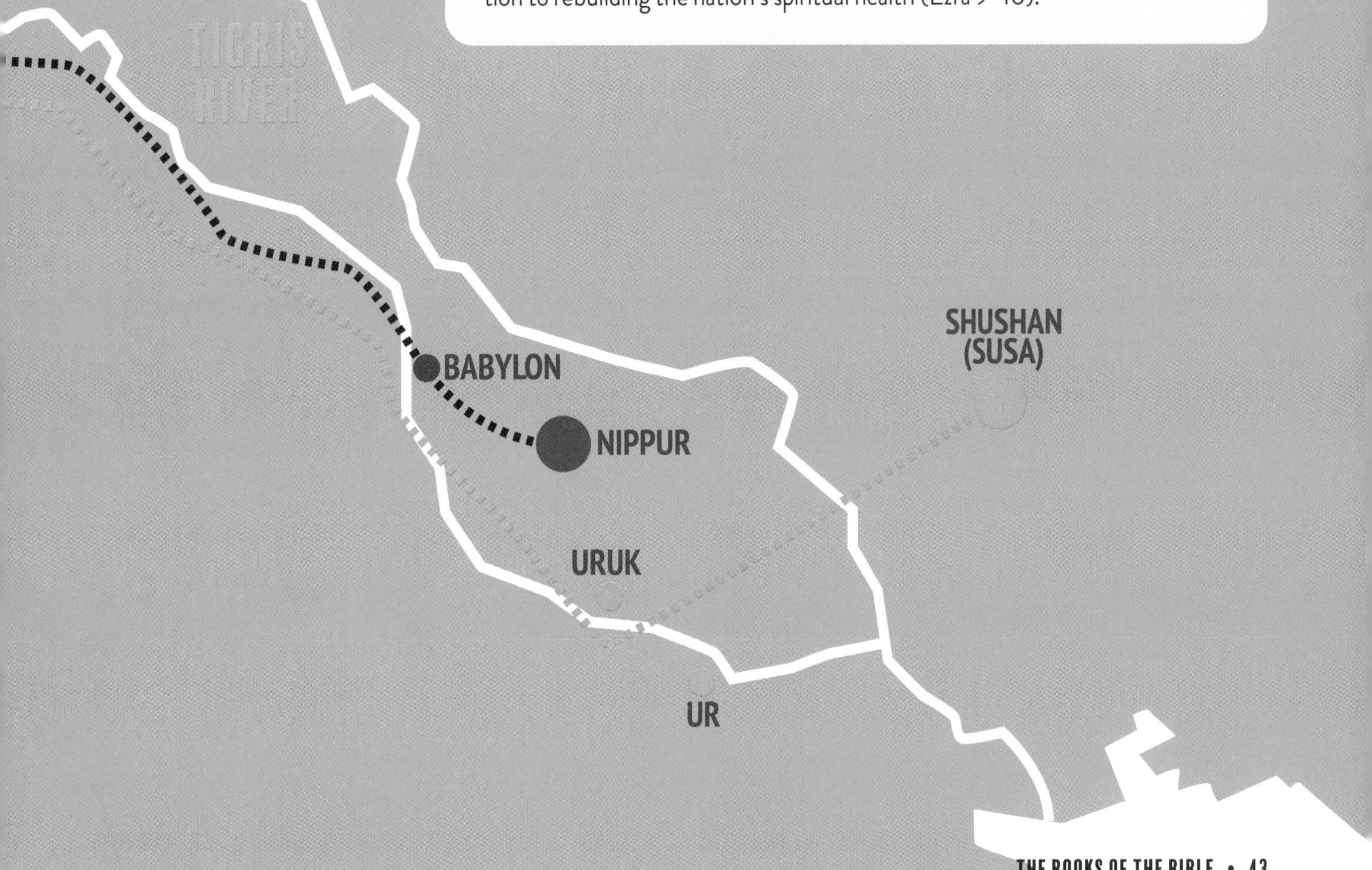

TIGRIS RIVER

BABYLON

NIPPUR

SHUSHAN (SUSA)

URUK

UR

NEHEMIAH:
BUILDING THE WALLS OF JERUSALEM

After receiving permission from King Artaxerxes of Persia in 444 BC, Nehemiah made the long journey to Jerusalem. Upon arriving, he surveyed the broken-down walls and quickly began to organize work groups to repair the wall in sections. The wall stretched from the Temple Mount area in the north part of the city to the southern end of the city of David. This wall, which had several access gates, surrounded all of Jerusalem with a barrier that gave God's people added protection from their enemies.

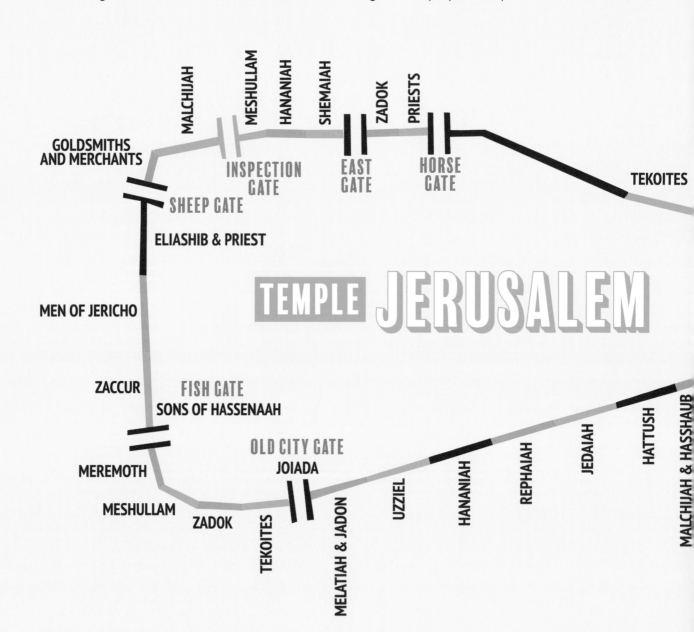

MALCHIJAH
MESHULLAM
HANANIAH
SHEMAIAH
ZADOK
PRIESTS

GOLDSMITHS AND MERCHANTS

INSPECTION GATE

EAST GATE

HORSE GATE

TEKOITES

SHEEP GATE

ELIASHIB & PRIEST

MEN OF JERICHO

TEMPLE JERUSALEM

ZACCUR

FISH GATE
SONS OF HASSENAAH

OLD CITY GATE
JOIADA

HATTUSH

JEDAIAH

REPHAIAH

HANANIAH

UZZIEL

MALCHIJAH & HASSHAUB

MEREMOTH

MESHULLAM
ZADOK
TEKOITES
MELATIAH & JADON

QUICK FACTS

- Forty-one groups were assigned a section of the wall to work on (Nehemiah 3:1-32).
- All the laborers were soldier-workers ready to defend themselves (4:16-18).
- At any given time, half the men were standing guard while the other half worked on the wall (4:21).
- The wall was completed in 52 days (6:15).
- In seven months, the people were in the city and towns (6:15; 7:73).

- Nehemiah ruled Jerusalem as governor for 12 years (5:14).
- The surrounding nations feared Israel (6:16).
- All the leaders of Israel lived in Jerusalem (11:1).
- Though Jerusalem was "wide and large," the city was unpopulated because the houses were still in ruins (7:4). So the people cast lots to see who would live in the city (11:1).
- More than 50,000 Israelites lived in and around Jerusalem (7:66-67).

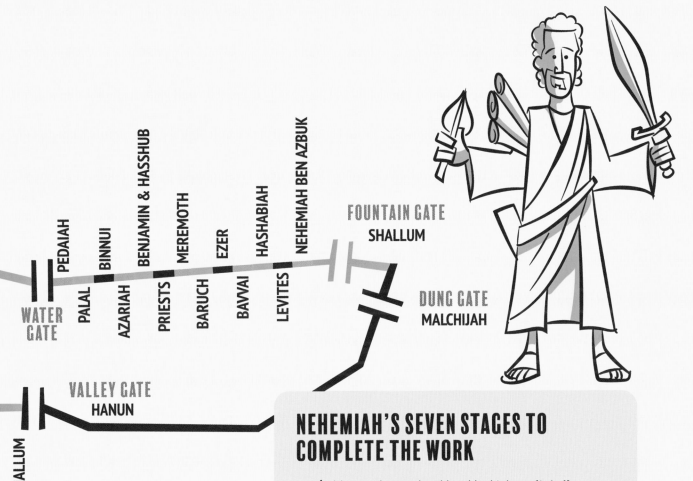

NEHEMIAH'S SEVEN STAGES TO COMPLETE THE WORK

1. He *sees* the need and *humbles his heart* (1:4-6)
2. He *acts* to bring about change (2:1-8)
3. He *surveys* the damage (2:9-16)
4. He *organizes* the people (2:17-20)
5. He *defends* against opposition (4:1–5:14)
6. He *completes* the wall (5:15)
7. He *blesses* the Israelites (7–13)

ESTHER: ESTHER SAVES HER PEOPLE

After the Persian king Cyrus freed the Jewish exiles from captivity in Babylon, many Israelites remained in the region and subsequently settled in Susa, Persia, during the reign of King Ahasuerus (485–464 BC), who was also known by his Greek name, Xerxes I. Esther (her name means "star") was a beautiful Jewish woman who became the queen in Persia and bravely saved her people from imminent destruction. The book of Esther is a story of redemption.

OUTLINE OF EVENTS

1 Esther is raised by her cousin Mordecai (Esther 2:7)

2 King Ahasuerus divorces Queen Vashti (1:10-22)

3 The search begins for a new queen (2:1-14)

4 Esther finds favor and becomes queen of the Persian Empire (2:15-18)

5 Because Mordecai refuses to bow to Haman the Agagite, Haman plots to kill Mordecai and all the Jews (3:1-6, 12-13)

6 Mordecai and Esther discover Haman's plot (4:1-16)

7 Esther bravely approaches the king with a plea to save her people (5:1-8; 8:1-14)

8 Haman and his sons are executed (7:7-10; 9:6-22)

9 By royal decree, the Jews in Persia destroy 75,000 of their persecutors (9:16)

10 The celebratory holiday of Purim is instituted (9:20-28)

KEY VERSES: "Who knows whether you have not come to the kingdom for such a time as this?...I will go to the king...and if I perish, I perish" (Esther 4:14-16).

WHO WAS HAMAN?

Haman was an Agagite (Esther 3:1); he was a descendent of King Agag of the Amalekites. Nearly 600 years earlier, God had instructed the Israelite king Saul to destroy all the Amalekites in Canaan (1 Samuel 15:1-3). But Saul disobeyed and spared some of the Amalekites, including King Agag (1 Samuel 15:9). This allowed Agag to have descendants (including Haman). These descendants were the ones who nearly annihilated all the Jews living in Persia when Esther was queen. Saul's failure demonstrates that disobeying God can have disastrous consequences.

GOD'S NAME IS HIDDEN IN THE BOOK OF ESTHER

Verse	Speaker	Acrostic Passage	Direction	Hebrew Word
1:20	Menucan	...all women will give...	Backward	YHWH— *Yahweh*
5:4	Esther	...let the king and Haman come today...	Forward	HWHY— *Yahweh*
5:13	Haman	...this is worth nothing...	Backward	YHWH— *Yahweh*
7:7	Author	...that harm was determined against him...	Forward	HWHY—*Yahweh*
7:5	Ahasuerus	Who is he, and where is he...	Forward	EHYH—I AM

*The acrostics are contained in the first or last letter of four consecutive words and can be spelled backward or forward (e.g., YHWH or HWHY). All are the Hebrew tetragrammaton YHWH except for Esther 7:5.

QUICK FACTS

- King Ahasuerus reigned over 127 provinces; his empire stretched from India in the east to Ethiopia in the west.
- God's name is not mentioned in the book of Esther.
- God's providential care of his people is seen throughout the book.
- The book of Esther has two parts: Chapters 1–4 describe the *threat* to the Jews; chapters 5–10 show the *deliverance* of the Jews.
- The feast of King Ahasuerus is described in chapters 1–4, while the feast of Queen Esther and Purim are mentioned in chapters 5–10.
- The chronological span of the book is ten years and fits between chapters 6 and 7 of Ezra.
- Esther is a Persian name; the queen's birth name was Hadassah, which means "myrtle" (2:7).
- Esther was an orphan (2:7).

JOB: SUFFERING, FAITHFULNESS, AND RESTORATION

Job was a righteous man who lived in the land of Uz (the region of Mesopotamia). He feared God and despised evil (Job 1:1). The devil wanted to show God that Job was only a "fair-weather friend" because of the abundant wealth God had given to Job. God knew Job's faithfulness was not anchored in his wealth; even so, God permitted the devil to test Job. The book describes Job's attempts to understand his suffering in light of God's existence, a topic that theologians call "theodicy." After Job had suffered greatly and lost his family, health, and wealth, God restored double of everything to Job.

JOB'S SEARCH FOR ANSWERS ABOUT HIS SUFFERING

KEY QUESTION: *Is God just in light of my suffering?*

Person	Scripture	The Argument	Focus	Conclusion
Job	Job 2–31; 27:2; 29:31; 31:35	"I have done nothing wrong."	"My suffering is unfair and not divine justice."	Job demands an explanation from God.
Job's Wife	Job 2:9	"Curse God and die."	Morality is foolish and God is unjust in light of Job's suffering.	God doesn't care and is unworthy of devotion.
Job's Three Friends: Eliphaz, Bildad, Zophar	Job 3–28	God must be just.	Job must be a moral failure.	Because God is just, Job is surely being punished for some sin he has committed.
Elihu	Job 32–37	God is just.	God governs the world according to justice.	Suffering is God's wake-up call to Job and builds character.
God's Response to Job	Job 38–41	God has an infinite perspective of the world, while Job's understanding is limited.	The distinction between God's and man's vantage points makes Job unqualified to judge God.	The world is good, but not perfect. Suffering is unavoidable. God has good purposes for suffering even if Job is not aware of them.
God's Response to Job's Friends	Job 42:7-9	"After the LORD had spoken these words to Job, the LORD said to Eliphaz the Temanite: 'My anger burns against you and against your two friends, for you have not spoken of me what is right, as my servant Job has. Now therefore take seven bulls and seven rams and go to my servant Job and offer up a burnt offering for yourselves. And my servant Job shall pray for you, for I will accept his prayer not to deal with you according to your folly. For you have not spoken of me what is right, as my servant Job has.' So Eliphaz the Temanite and Bildad the Shuhite and Zophar the Naamathite went and did what the LORD had told them, and the LORD accepted Job's prayer."		

CONCLUSION: Because God is all-knowing, all-powerful, and all-loving, we should have faith in God's wisdom, purposes, and plans even if we don't understand them.

THEODICY A CHRISTIAN PERSPECTIVE OF EVIL

Where did evil come from?	Evil originated when Lucifer misused his freedom and exalted himself over God. Evil entered the physical world when Adam and Eve disobeyed God and ate of the forbidden fruit in the garden of Eden.
If God created all things, does that mean God created evil?	No. Even though evil is real, evil, in itself, is not a material *thing*. Rather, it is a lack or absence of what should be present in good things (such as a hole in a shirt). God made evil *possible* by giving us free will, but man makes evil *actual* by choices.
Is God the author of evil (Isaiah 45:7)?	God does not author evil in the sense of sin and moral perversity, but is the author of calamity, plagues, and chastisement, which are viewed as "evils" to the one experiencing them (such as the plagues upon Pharaoh and the Egyptians in the book of Exodus).
Does God will evil?	God doesn't will or not will evil. He doesn't *promote* it, but simply *permits* evil to occur.
Is God to blame for evil?	No. God gave mankind the *potential* to do evil through free choice; therefore, people are responsible for their own decisions. To blame God would be like blaming Henry Ford, instead of individual drivers, for all auto accidents because Ford helped to make automobiles possible.
Why doesn't God destroy evil now?	God destroyed evil *positionally* by dying on the cross and will destroy evil *practically* at his second coming. If God were to remove all evil immediately, He would also have to remove human free will, which is the means by which we receive salvation. So we must be patient for the time when God brings all evil to an end.
Are there benefits we can derive from the effects of evil?	Yes. Ministry and servanthood are possible only when there is a lack (evil). There is no courage without danger, no perseverance without obstacles, and no gain without pain. In addition, many of the most valuable lessons in life are learned through times of adversity.
Are there purposes in pain and suffering?	Yes, pain can often preserve us from greater problems (such as the dentist's drill); we show compassion and comfort to others because we are aware of the need for these through our own experiences. God can use evil to fulfill his purposes and plans. For example, Joseph said to his brothers that the cruelty they showed toward him was meant for evil, but God meant it for good to help keep many people alive during a severe famine (Genesis 50:20).
If God is perfect, why does this world have evil in it?	God permits evil temporarily to bring about a greater good for mankind. That is to say, if Adam and Eve hadn't sinned, they would have lived under the constant threat of potentially falling into sin and potentially dying as a result. Even before they sinned, God had designed a plan to remove the threat of evil permanently so that we will be better off in the end (in heaven) without the potential to ever sin or die. While we are not in the best of all possible worlds right now, what we are experiencing is the best way to get to the best of all possible worlds as long as humans still have free will.
Could God have avoided evil?	Yes, he could have created us with no free will, but that would make us nothing more than robots who must do what God programs us to do. This would make love, praise, and obedience totally meaningless. People would have no moral responsibility; hence, no reward or punishment. Perhaps God could have not created anything at all, but to go down that path is to say that nothing is better than something. Common sense agrees that a half of a loaf of bread is better than no loaf at all. To have something is better than to have nothing, even if there is risk involved.

PSALMS: THE LANGUAGE OF PRAYER AND PRAISE

The psalms are a collection of 150 chapters (poems), written from 1450–430 BC by multiple authors. These writings emphasize prayers and praises to God and are often referred to as a hymnbook because of how the psalms are used in the church for musical lyrics, as well as the use of the word *song* (Greek *psalmos*; Hebrew *mizmor*) in many of the psalm titles. The Hebrew Bible titles the book *Tehillim*, which means "praises."

STRUCTURE OF THE PSALMS

	Book 1	Book 2	Book 3	Book 4	Book 5
Psalms	1–41	42–72	73–89	90–106	107–150
Author	David	Mostly David, sons of Korah, Solomon (1)	Mostly Asaph and sons of Korah	Mostly anonymous, David (2), Moses (1)	David, Solomon (1), anonymous
Type	Lament/enemies	Lament/enemies	Mostly corporate praise and lament	Praise	Hallelujah/songs of ascent, pilgrimage psalms
Theme	David flees from Saul	David as king	The Assyrian invasion	Thoughts of the destruction of the temple and exile to Babylon	Praise for returning from exile and restoration
Contents	Personal	Devotional	Historical	General	Prophetic
Emphasis	Humanity	Deliverance	Sanctuary	Kingdom of God	Word of God
Key Psalm	Psalms 22–23	Psalm 45:6-7	Psalm 84	Psalm 103	Psalm 119
Key Verse	"My mouth will speak the praise of the LORD, and let all flesh bless his holy name forever and ever" (Psalm 145:21).				

TEN LITERARY TYPES OF PSALMS

1 **Lament psalms** (Psalm 12)—prayers of deliverance

2 **Imprecatory psalms** (Psalm 10:15)—call upon God's wrath/judgment upon God's enemies out of righteous indignation

3 **Wisdom psalms** (Psalm 37)—practical advice for godly living

4 **Royal psalms** (Psalm 2)—expectations of messianic rule

5 **Thanksgiving psalms** (Psalm 30)—offerings of thanks to God and emphasizing his greatness

6 **Pilgrimage psalms** (Psalm 107–150)—songs to sing during the journeys to Jerusalem to celebrate the feasts

7 **Enthronement psalms** (Psalms 49; 93; 96–99)—emphasize God's sovereignty, rule, and reign

8 **Confidence psalms** (Psalm 23)—emphasize a deep trust in God during difficult times

9 **Historical psalms** (Psalm 78)—corporate songs that focus on a lesson from history through which God worked among the people in some tangible way

10 **Celebratory psalms that extol God's law and Word** (Psalm 119)—songs that praise the Scriptures and God's law

QUICK FACTS ABOUT THE PSALMS

- Psalms is the largest book in the poetry section of the Bible. Because of this, Jesus used the title of the book to refer to the entire body of poetry books (Luke 24:44).

- David wrote the most psalms (73). After that are psalms written by Asaph (12), the sons of Korah (11), Solomon (2), and Moses (1).

- The psalms emphasize various themes, such as monotheism, covenants, election, creation, messianic rule, the Word of God, and the end times.

- The meaning of the often-repeated term *Selah* is uncertain. It may have served as some sort of musical direction for those leading or singing the song.

- Among the Dead Sea Scrolls, Psalm 151 was discovered, which is included in the text of the Septuagint (or LXX, which is the Greek translation of the Hebrew Bible) but is missing from the Hebrew Masoretic Text that was used as the basis for the English Bible. It is considered by most to be an uninspired psalm that is noncanonical.

PROVERBS: WORDS OF WISDOM

ABOUT THE BOOK OF PROVERBS

AUTHORS: King Solomon (Proverbs 1–29), Agur (Proverbs 30), and Lemuel (Proverbs 31)

DATE: 950–700 BC

LOCATION: Judah

THEME: Imparting wisdom to God's people so they can live a skillful life in the fear of the Lord

PRINCIPLE: Think before you act

CHAPTERS: 31

VERSES: 915

LANGUAGE: Hebrew

GENRE: Wisdom literature

TYPE: Hebrew parallelism

The book of Proverbs comprises part of the wisdom section of the Old Testament along with Esther, Job, Psalms, Ecclesiastes, and Song of Solomon. The Hebrew Scriptures place the proverbs in the section titled *Ketuvim* (the Writings). Proverbs offers wisdom and life lessons for God's people; they are grounded in the fear of the Lord and they are simple, concise sayings (Proverbs 1:1-7; 9:10). The title *Proverbs* means "words that go before"—that is, the principles imparted should *lead* your life choices and serve as the beginning of right thoughts and behaviors.

STRUCTURE OF PROVERBS

Chapters	Proverbs 1:1-7	Proverbs 1:8–9:18	Proverbs 10–29	Proverbs 30–31
Section	Introduction	Invitation	Proverbs	Precepts
Emphasis	Beginning of wisdom	People of wisdom	Principles of wisdom	Practice of wisdom
Author	Solomon	Solomon	Solomon	Agur/Lemuel
Key Verses	1:7	3:5-6	14:12	30:4
Theme	"Trust in the LORD with all your heart, and do not lean on your own understanding. In all your ways acknowledge him, and he will make straight your paths" (Proverbs 3:5-6).			

TYPES OF PROVERBS

Under the inspiration of the Holy Spirit, Solomon used Hebrew parallelism to communicate his wisdom principles. There are three basic kinds of this type of communication: (1) REPETITION, (2) CONTRAST, and (3) COMPLETION.

REPETITIOUS PARALLELISM—Also called synonymous parallelism, the second line of the proverb repeats the principle of the first line using different words (Proverbs 1:2; 16:18).

CONTRASTING PARALLELISM—Also called antithetical parallelism, the second line of the proverb states the principle of the first line by using a contrasting statement (Proverbs 10:1).

COMPLETING PARALLELISM—Also called synthetic parallelism, the second line of the proverb completes the broad thought stated in the first line with a specific truth, thus expanding our knowledge of the principle (Proverbs 16:4).

ABOUT SOLOMON

- He was the son of King David and his wife Bathsheba
- He was the third king of Israel and ruled for 40 years (971–931 BC)
- His reign marked the height of the kingdom of Israel
- He was the last king to reign over all of Israel (north and south)
- He asked God for wisdom to rule his people and received it (1 Kings 3:9-12)
- He didn't ask for riches, but God gave them to him anyway
- He was the wisest person who ever lived (besides Jesus)
- People came from all over the world to hear his wisdom
- He was not perfect; he had multiple wives and set up altars to foreign gods (1 Kings 10:26; 11:1)
- He spoke 3,000 proverbs and wrote 1,005 songs (1 Kings 4:32)
- He wrote the books of Ecclesiastes and the Song of Solomon
- He wrote Psalms 72 and 127
- His proverbs in chapters 25–29 were collected and copied by King Hezekiah's court (25:1)
- He built the first Jewish temple to the Lord

TELLING THE DIFFERENCE

IDIOMS—These are words that don't literally mean what they say. For example, the saying, "Flesh and blood cannot inherit the kingdom of God" (1 Corinthians 15:50) means *mortality* cannot exist in heaven. Thus, a person needs to be made immortal by the resurrection.

ADAGES—These are expressions that refer to how people think or behave. For example, the expression "You can't have your cake and eat it too" refers to someone who wants two contradictory options to be true but must pick one or the other.

PROVERBS—These are sayings that offer wise advice, guiding principles, or instructions about a specific way to live or think about your life and relationship to others. For example, "My son, if sinners entice you, do not consent" (Proverbs 1:10).

ECCLESIASTES:
FINDING MEANING UNDER THE SUN

The book of Ecclesiastes records the words of the "Preacher" (Hebrew *Qoheleth*), telling of his many experiences in life as he seeks to find meaning and satisfaction in the things we do here on earth. He analyzes life as if he were conducting a scientific experiment, testing hypotheses and then forming conclusions as to whether, in the end, life brings fulfillment. Apparently, he found nothing meaningful or satisfying "under the sun" (mentioned 29 times), seeing everything as "vanity" (empty and without substance; Ecclesiastes 1:2-3). Only when a person looks "above the sun" and sees these same experiences in light of an eternal perspective does life become meaningful and satisfying.

AUTHOR

Though Solomon's name is not mentioned in the book, the identity of "the Preacher" can be deduced from Ecclesiastes 1:1, 12. Because there has been only one "son of David" who was "king over Israel in Jerusalem," the writer must be Solomon. No other king after Solomon could make this claim due to the kingdom being divided immediately after Solomon's reign.

DATE

Some scholars attempt to date Ecclesiastes to 350–250 BC because of the presence of some Aramaic and Persian words. However, Bible scholar Gleason Archer has shown these words to be similar to the Phoenician and Canaanite words that predate Solomon. Therefore, the best date is ca. 950–930 BC.

OUTLINE OF ECCLESIASTES

Chapters	Theme	Focus	Approach	Conclusion
1–2	Searching for meaning in life	Declaration of vanity	Seek and explore by wisdom	Emptiness abounds in life and nature
3–5	Finding meaning in life	Demonstration of vanity	Personal pursuits	Ultimately, nothing satisfies
6–7	Examining meaning in life	Deliverance from vanity	Wisdom for living	Making sense of life
8–12	Possessing meaning in life	Overcoming vanity	Wisdom for living and conclusion of the search	Fear God and keep his commandments, for everything will be judged
Key Word	"Vanity" (Hebrew *hebel*) is used 37 times and means "vapor," referring to the emptiness that results from seeking satisfaction apart from God.			
Key Phrase	"Under the sun" is used 31 times and refers to this temporal, fallen, natural world in which we live (1:3). "Above the sun" refers to a heavenly perspective of life.			
Key Verse	"What does man gain by all the toil at which he toils under the sun?" (1:3).			
Christ	Ecclesiastes 12:11—Christ is the "one Shepherd" who gives us a unified message that both pricks (goads) our hearts to move in a direction we otherwise would avoid and gives us stability and security (nails).			

SONG of SOLOMON
A SONG FOR THE BELOVED

The Song of Solomon (sometimes called the Song of Songs) is the greatest of Solomon's 1,005 songs he wrote between 965–931 BC (1 Kings 4:32). The book has been interpreted a variety of ways, but it clearly presents a romantic courtship between a shepherd and a shepherdess (1:1-8). Some suggest that the shepherd is Solomon, and that he authored the book describing his own personal experience (1:1). Others believe the Song was written by an unknown author in Solomon's honor. Either way, the book emphasizes the joy and intimacy of love within the marriage relationship and foreshadows Christ's loving and intimate relationship with the church, his bride (Song of Solomon 2:4, 16; Ephesians 5:22-32).

OUTLINE

CHAPTERS 1–3: The COURTSHIP of the bride and groom

CHAPTERS 3–4: The MARRIAGE of the bride and groom

CHAPTERS 5–8: The MATURING of the bride and groom

KEY VERSE:

"Many waters cannot quench love, neither can floods drown it. If a man offered for love all the wealth of his house, he would be utterly despised" (Song of Solomon 8:7).

QUICK FACTS

- The book has eight chapters and 117 verses
- The book uses nearly 50 unique words not found anywhere else in the Bible
- Solomon addresses love, companionship, union, marriage, pleasure, separation, praise, and attraction
- The book is written as a love song
- Solomon alludes to 21 species of plants, 15 species of animals, and 15 geographical regions
- The "Shulamite" shepherdess may be from Shunem, located near the Sea of Galilee in northern Israel

WHAT IS THE LOVE COMMANDMENT?

Jesus said the greatest commandment is to love God with all our heart, soul, mind, and strength, and the second greatest is to love our neighbor as ourselves (Matthew 22:36-39). Jesus later said that obeying these commandments fulfills all the commands that "the Law and the Prophets" presented (Matthew 22:40). These two commands inform us how we should relate vertically to God and horizontally to people—we should do so in love. This means that the core of our duty to God and to others is grounded in love. All of our decisions should start, and end, and be guided by love.

WHAT DOES THE BIBLE SAY ABOUT LOVE?

The Bible uses different Greek words to speak of love; each word has its own unique emphasis:

- PHILEO—brotherly love, fondness, and friendship (John 11:3, 36)
- EROS—although this Greek word is not used in the Bible, the concept of intimate love in a committed marriage relationship is present (Song of Solomon 7:6)
- STORGE—the natural, heartfelt fondness and affection for one's own son or daughter (Romans 12:10; 2 Timothy 3:3)
- AGAPE—unconditional and preferential love that is chosen; the kind of love God has for us and we should have for him and each other (John 13:35; Romans 5:8)

ISAIAH: THE FIRST OF THE MAJOR PROPHETS

The book of Isaiah is first in a sequence of several books that comprise what are known as the major prophets, along with Jeremiah, Daniel, and Ezekiel. The term *major* refers to the lengths of these books, whereas the shorter books are designated as the minor prophets. Isaiah's ministry endured through the reigns of four Judean kings—Uzziah, Jotham, Ahaz, and Hezekiah— beginning in 740 BC and ending in 680 BC. His message is largely messianic in nature, describing the suffering servant and his coming kingdom, as well as addressing the Assyrian invasion threat, and addressing judgement oracles to various nations.

QUICK FACTS

- Isaiah's name means "Yahweh is salvation."
- Isaiah's ministry continued for 60 years.
- The word *salvation* is mentioned 26 times, but only seven times in all the other prophetic books combined.
- Isaiah prophesied that Babylon would judge Judah nearly 100 years before Babylon became a superpower.
- The book has 66 chapters and 1,292 verses.
- Isaiah has 130 messianic prophecies.
- In the same way that the Bible has 66 books total, with 39 in the Old Testament and 27 in the New, Isaiah has 66 chapters, with 39 in the first section and 27 in the second.
- After chapter 39, Isaiah's name does not appear in the book.

OUTLINE OF ISAIAH

Chapters	1–35	36–39	40–55	56–66
Setting	Oracles against the nations and the eighth-century BC Assyrian invasion	Historical bridge of transition— Hezekiah's blessing	The sixth-century BC Babylonian exile and the Suffering Servant	Prophecies of Israel's glorious future
Kings	Uzziah, Jotham, Ahaz (740–715 BC)	Hezekiah (715–686 BC)	Hezekiah	Hezekiah
Location	Jerusalem	Jerusalem	Jerusalem	Jerusalem
Actions	Purification of Israel through Assyrian judgment		God comforts his people in exile	God prepares his people for the coming redemption
Themes	God's judgment and holy character		God's exclusive glory revealed	Justice/righteousness
Key Verses	6:1-13		44:6	53:5

KEY VERSE: "Though he had done so many signs before them, they still did not believe in him, so that the word spoken by the prophet Isaiah might be fulfilled: 'Lord, who has believed what he heard from us, and to whom has the arm of the Lord been revealed?'" (John 12:37-38; citing Isaiah 53:1).

WHAT DID THE MESSIAH SUFFER?

He was not desired (53:2)
He was despised (verse 3)
He was rejected (verse 3)
He was acquainted with grief (verse 3)
He was not esteemed (verse 3)
He was the bearer of griefs (verse 4)
He carried our sorrows (verse 4)
He was stricken (verse 4)
He was afflicted (verse 4)
He was wounded/bruised (verse 5)

He was crushed (verse 5)
He was chastised (verse 5)
He was scourged (verse 5)
He carried our iniquity (verse 6)
He was oppressed (verse 7)
He was silent (verse 7)
He was like a lamb led to slaughter (verse 7)
He was cut off from the living (verse 8)
He was stricken for transgression (verse 8)
He was taken (verse 8)

He was killed with the wicked (verse 9)
He did no violence (verse 9)
He was silent (verse 9)
He had no deceit (verse 9)
He was buried (verse 9)
He was an offering for sin (verse 10)
He was poured out (verse 12)
He was numbered with the transgressors (verse 12)

TIMELINE OF THE PROPHETS

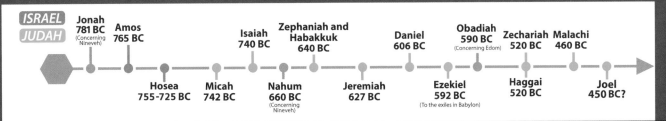

ISRAEL
JUDAH

Jonah 781 BC (Concerning Nineveh)
Amos 765 BC
Isaiah 740 BC
Zephaniah and Habakkuk 640 BC
Daniel 606 BC
Obadiah 590 BC (Concerning Edom)
Zechariah 520 BC
Malachi 460 BC

Hosea 755-725 BC
Micah 742 BC
Nahum 660 BC (Concerning Nineveh)
Jeremiah 627 BC
Ezekiel 592 BC (To the exiles in Babylon)
Haggai 520 BC
Joel 450 BC?

BEFORE THE EXILE | DURING THE EXILE | AFTER THE EXILE

20 NORTHERN KINGS

JEROBOAM 931–910 BC
NADAB 910–909 BC
BAASHA 909–886 BC
ELAH 886–885 BC
ZIMRI 885 BC
TIBNI 885–880 BC
OMRI 885–874 BC
AHAB 874–853 BC
AHAZIAH 853–852 BC
JORAM (JEHORAM) 852–841 BC
JEHU 841–814 BC
JEHOAHAZ 814–798 BC
JEHOASH 798–782 BC
JEROBOAM II 793–753BC
ZECHARIAH 753 BC
SHALLUM 752 BC
MENAHEM 752–742 BC
PEKAHIAH 742–740 BC
PEKAH 752–732 BC
HOSHEA 732–722 BC

20 SOUTHERN KINGS

REHOBOAM 931–913 BC
ABIJAH 913–911 BC
ASA 911–870 BC
JEHOSHAPHAT 873–848 BC
JEHORAM (JORAM) 853–841 BC
AHAZIAH 841 BC
QUEEN ATHALIAH 841–835 BC
JOASH 835–796 BC
AMAZIAH 796–767 BC
UZZIAH (AZARIAH) 792–740 BC
JOTHAM 750–722 BC
AHAZ (JEHOAHAZ) 735–716 BC
HEZEKIAH 716–687 BC
MANASSEH 697–643 BC
AMON 643–641 BC
JOSIAH 641–609 BC
JEHOAHAZ (SHALLUM) 609 BC
JEHOIAKIM (ELIAKIM) 609–598 BC
JEHOIACHIN (JECONIAH) 598–597 BC
ZEDEKIAH (MATTANIAH) 597–586 BC

THE SUFFERING SERVANT

Chapter 53 is an important messianic section of the book of Isaiah. Here, Isaiah prophesies, in the past tense, more than 700 years *before* Christ was born the suffering that the Lord would endure in order to bear the sins of Israel and the world.

JEREMIAH: THE COMING CAPTIVITY

Jeremiah, sometimes called the weeping prophet, prophesied and was an eyewitness to the Babylonian captivity in 586 BC. His 42-year ministry (627–586 BC), spanning the reigns of kings Josiah, Jehoahaz, Jehoiakim, Jehoiachin, and Zedekiah, was a tough journey culminating in Judah's captivity. Though Jeremiah ministered for a long time, only two people came to God as a result: Baruch, his scribe (32:12; 36:1-4), and the Ethiopian eunuch Ebed-melech, who served the king (38:7-13; 39:15-18). Among his animated prophecies (he once wore an ox yoke to symbolize captivity) to the Judean leadership was God's promise of a new covenant with his people Israel and Judah (31:33). Interestingly, the prophet Daniel cites Jeremiah 25:11-12 as the period of time (70 years) God's people will be in Babylonian exile (cf. Daniel 9:2).

OUTLINE

1. Introduction and Israel's unfaithfulness (1–6)
2. Israel's idolatry (7–10)
3. Jeremiah's suffering and opposition (11–20)
4. Jeremiah confronts kings and people (21–29)
5. God will restore his people (30–33)
6. God judges his people (34–45)
7. God judges other nations (46–51)
8. Judah's fall and exile (52)

QUICK FACTS

- Jeremiah had a scribe named Baruch, the son of Neriah, write his book for him (Jeremiah 36:1-32)
- The overseer of the temple complex in Jerusalem, Pashhur, had Jeremiah beaten and placed in stocks (20:2)
- Jeremiah was cast into a pit (38:6)
- After the Babylonian invasion, Jeremiah was released from his chains by a military officer named Nebuzaradan (40:1)
- Jeremiah was taken to Egypt (43)

SERIOUSLY?

CHAPTERS/EVENTS

KINGS/DATES	CHAPTERS/EVENTS
Josiah (627–609 BC)	1:1-19; 3:6–6:30
Jehoahaz and Jehoiakim (609–597 BC)	7; 25; 26; 35–36; 45–48
Johoiachin and Zedekiah (597–586 BC)	20–22; 24; 27–30; 32–34; 37–39; 49–52
Gedaliah, governor of Judah (after 586 BC)	40–44

KEY VERSES:
"As it is, Christ has obtained a ministry that is as much more excellent than the old as the covenant he mediates is better, since it is enacted on better promises. For if that first covenant had been faultless, there would have been no occasion to look for a second" (Hebrews 8:6-7).

"I will give you a new heart, and a new spirit I will put within you. And I will remove the heart of stone from your flesh and give you a heart of flesh" (Ezekiel 36:26).

COMPARING THE TWO COVENANTS

(2 Corinthians 3:1-18; Colossians 2:15-23)

The old covenant between God and his people was given by Moses while Israel was in the wilderness. This covenant was based on obedience to the letter of the law. Jeremiah predicted a time when a new covenant would be given to God's people through the Messiah, Jesus Christ. Moses and the prophets also wrote of a time when Israel would fail to live up to the old covenant (Deuteronomy 30:1-8). There are many differences between the two covenants, as seen in the comparisons here.

OLD COVENANT	NEW COVENANT
Blood of animals	Blood of Christ
Shadow	Substance
Powerless to save from sin	Power to save from sin
Temporal	Eternal
Written with ink	Written with the Spirit
Insufficient	Sufficient
Written on stone	Written on the heart
Annual atonement	Eternal atonement
The letter kills	The Spirit gives life
Ministry of death	Ministry of the Spirit
Had fading glory	Has lasting glory
Brought condemnation	Brings righteousness
Had a veil when reading the covenant	Veil is removed in Christ
The heart is veiled in Moses	Veil is removed when interpreted through Christ
Bondage	Liberty
The former was dependent upon the glory of Moses	The latter leads to transformation to the glory of Christ
Focus is obedience	Focus is the heart, which leads to obedience
Emphasis is on fulfilling ceremonial works	Emphasis is on relationship with Christ

LAMENTATIONS:
JERUSALEM IN MOURNING

The book of Lamentations describes the suffering and mourning in Jerusalem following the Babylonian invasion and destruction of the city. Some see the book as a funeral-like postscript to the book of Jeremiah. Arranged around five acrostic poems that follow the 22 letters of the Hebrew alphabet, each chapter describes Jerusalem in various ways. Some believe Jeremiah authored the book, while others believe it was composed by an eyewitness of these events sometime between 586–516 BC.

THE MESSAGE OF LAMENTATIONS

CHAPTER 1

Jerusalem Suffers and Cries Out (1:1)

The city is described as a grieving widow, devastated by depopulation and an infrastructure in ruins. The princes have become slaves and Israel's enemies now rule (1:1-11). Jerusalem cries out for help (verses 12-22).

CHAPTER 2

The Lord Places Jerusalem Under a Cloud (2:1)

The Lord has become like an enemy to his people. Jerusalem's splendor has been destroyed and its protective strongholds pulled down. All of this has multiplied Judah's mourning (2:1-19). This causes those in Jerusalem to call upon God to see their plight and to act on their behalf (verses 20-22).

CHAPTER 3

God's Punishment Should Lead to Hope (3:38-41)

From an eyewitness perspective of one who is experiencing the suffering, the writer holds out hope for prayer and spiritual renewal and that God will not forget his people (3:1-47). In light of the deplorable circumstances, the people are exhorted to maintain confidence in God (verses 48-66).

CHAPTER 4

Describing a Desolate Jerusalem (4:11-12)

Jerusalem has become a shadow of itself, with children suffering (4:1-10), the punishment of religious leaders (verses 11-16; cf. 5:12), and Israel's enemies growing in strength (verses 17-20). However, the captors will be judged when Israel's punishment is complete (verses 20-22).

CHAPTER 5

A Plea for Restoration and Deliverance (5:1)

The final chapter begins with the petition "Remember, O LORD" (5:1), reciting the tragedy that has befallen Jerusalem (verses 2-18) and offers a concluding prayer for restoration (verses 19-22).

🔑 KEY VERSE: "The LORD has become like an enemy; he has swallowed up Israel; he has swallowed up all its palaces; he has laid in ruins its strongholds, and he has multiplied in the daughter of Judah mourning and lamentation" (Lamentations 2:5).

LIFE LESSON: No matter how bad things get, even after meting out punishment, our loving God never gives up on his people. He can restore what was destroyed and heal broken hearts and lives (Lamentations 3:24-25).

EZEKIEL: THE GLORY OF THE LORD

OUTLINE

1. The Lord judges his people (1–24)
2. The Lord judges the nations (25–32)
3. The sovereign Lord restores his people, the city, and the temple (33–48)

 KEY VERSE: "Then they shall know that I am the LORD their God, because I sent them into exile among the nations and then assembled them into their own land. I will leave none of them remaining among the nations anymore" (Ezekiel 39:28).

 KEY EVENTS

- Ezekiel, the son of Busi, is born ca. 623 BC during King Josiah's reign
- First Babylonian siege of Jerusalem in 605 BC
- Second Babylonian siege of Jerusalem in 597 BC
- Ezekiel taken to Babylon with King Jehoiachin as an exile in 597 BC
- Ezekiel is called as a prophet in the fifth year of Jehoiachin's exile (593–592 BC)
- Third and final Babylonian siege in 586 BC; Jerusalem and the temple destroyed
- Ezekiel not allowed to grieve over his wife's death
- Ezekiel gives his last dated prophecy about 571 BC (29:17)
- Though Jerusalem and the temple are destroyed, Ezekiel foretells of a new future temple and a new city named Jehovah-shammah (meaning "the Lord is there")
- Ezekiel dies among the Judean exiles in Babylon

CHRIST IN EZEKIEL

Ezekiel anticipates Christ as the restorer (37), shepherd (34:23), cleanser (36:24-33), and above all, the glory of God (1, 43).

Ezekiel 17:22-23: "Thus says the Lord GOD: 'I myself will take a sprig from the lofty top of the cedar and will set it out. I will break off from the topmost of its young twigs a tender one, and I myself will plant it on a high and lofty mountain. On the mountain height of Israel will I plant it, that it may bear branches and produce fruit and become a noble cedar.'"

The book of Ezekiel can seem like a complicated maze of prophecy, with visions and imagery that can challenge the Bible interpreter's skill. Getting a grasp on the book becomes easier by noting the book's threefold focus: (1) the judgment of God's people, (2) the judgment of the nations, and (3) the restoration of God's people. Ezekiel (which means "God strengthens") was a married priest (1:3; 24:15-24) who cared deeply about Jerusalem and the temple. He had much to say about the deterioration of the spiritual life of Judah and the leadership that had become corrupt and useless. National judgment was the means God used to purify the nation. Ezekiel witnessed all three Babylonian sieges of Jerusalem, and though he was eventually carried away into exile, he would bring a message of hope to God's people by pointing to a future day of restoration.

The wood of the vine (15)—people of Jerusalem are useless
God's unfaithful wife (16)—people of Jerusalem have become adulterous
Two eagles and a vine (17)—Jerusalem destroyed because of King Zedekiah's rebellion
Dross in the furnace (22:17-22)—God uses the Babylonian siege to pour out his fiery wrath on Jerusalem to purify his people
Two promiscuous sisters (23)—Samaria and Jerusalem are unfaithful sisters
The cooking pot (24:1-14)—Jerusalem's impurities and corrosion judged and purified
Mariners sink into the sea (27)—the judgment of Tyre will be like a shipwreck
The shepherds (34)—the leaders of Israel are useless
The dry bones (37:1-14)—Israel will be renewed and restored as one nation

THE BATTLE OF GOG AND MAGOG — *Ezekiel 38–39*

Ezekiel prophesied 2,600 years ago that in the last days (38:8, 16) a confederacy of nations will launch a major invasion of Israel and that God will supernaturally deliver his people against overwhelming odds. Many evangelical scholars have wondered about the timing of this conflict. Some say it could occur prior to the second coming of Christ. Others view the battle as taking place at the end of the millennial period (Revelation 20:7-9). What we can know for certain is this prophecy has yet to be fulfilled because there is no historical precedent for such an event. The reestablishment of Israel as a nation in 1948 (36:24), after more than 1,900 years of dispersion (since Jerusalem's destruction by the Romans in AD 70), is a prerequisite for this invasion to take place. The stage will be set for this epic battle to occur when Israel is at peace with its neighbors. Currently, Israel has signed peace treaties with Jordan and Egypt, and is working toward better relations with Saudi Arabia, an enemy of Iran.

CONFEDERACY OF NATIONS (38:1-6)

The confederacy of nations will be populated mostly by the descendants of ancient Japheth and Ham, who will attack the descendants of Shem (Israel) "like a cloud covering the land" (38:9).

ANCIENT NAME	MODERN NAME
Gog	Name or title of leader of the coalition of nations
Magog	Kazakhstan, Kyrgyzstan, Uzbekistan, Turkmenistan, Tajikistan, Afghanistan (lands north and east of Turkey)
Rosh (the remotest parts of the north)	Russia
Meshech, Tubal, Gomer, Beth-togarmah	Turkey (possibly with Azerbaijan and Armenia)
Persia	Iran
Cush	Ethiopia, Sudan
Put	Libya (possibly with Algeria and Tunisia)

CHARACTERISTICS
OF THE INVADING ARMY
(38:1-9, 15-16; 39:2, 4)

- Most of the army will come from the "uttermost parts of the north" (Russia and Turkey).
- The army will be massive, described as a "great host," "multitude," "hordes," and "like a cloud covering the land," "coming on like a storm."
- They will be well-equipped with full armor, horses, shields, bucklers, and swords.
- The epicenter of the battle will take place on the desolate mountains of Israel.
- The invading armies will be used by God to make known his holy name.

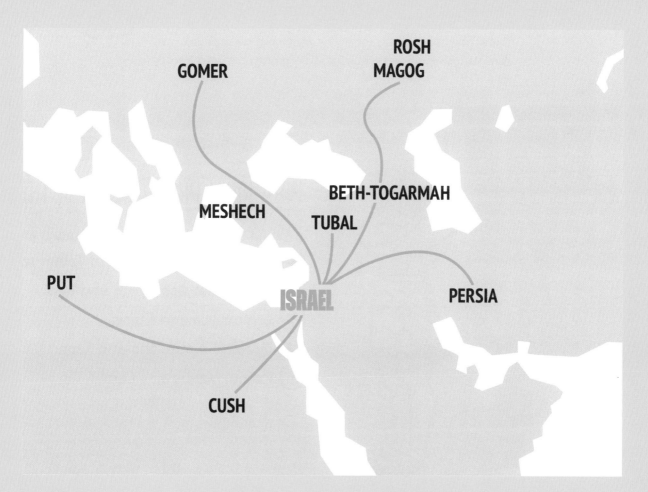

DANIEL: THE KEY TO PROPHECY

The book of Daniel presents several important prophecies regarding the Jewish people and their nation. Written in the sixth century BC, it not only records Daniel's experiences throughout the bulk of the Babylonian captivity (605–536 BC), it also offers a look forward in time to the successive kingdoms, as interpreted by Daniel, in King Nebuchadnezzar's vision of the metallic statue. In addition, Daniel (whose Babylonian name was Belteshazzar, 1:7) provides a specific time frame, known as the 70 Weeks of Daniel, for the arrival of the Messiah and his death, as well as the timing of the events that will take place during the tribulation period.

OUTLINE

1. Daniel and his three friends (1)
2. Nebuchadnezzar's dream and the prophetic history of the Gentile nations (2–7)
3. Prophetic history of Israel and Daniel's 70 weeks (8–12)

QUICK FACTS

Author: Daniel (means "God is my judge"); also known as Belteshazzar (means "protect the king")
Date: Sixth century BC
Language: Hebrew (1:1–2:3; 8:1–12:13) and Aramaic (2:4–7:28)
Location: Babylon
Theme: Prophecy, apocalyptic and future hope of redemption
Purpose: Demonstrates that God is sovereign over the kingdoms of men

DANIEL CHAPTER 2

GOLD
SILVER
BRONZE
IRON
IRON & CLAY

HISTORICAL PROGRESSION OF THE BABYLONIAN RELIGION

1. **Babylon:** Semiramis and Tammuz
2. **Phoenicia:** Ashtoreth and Baal
3. **Egypt:** Isis and Osiris
4. **Greece:** Aphrodite and Eros
5. **Rome:** Venus and Cupid

THE 70 WEEKS OF DANIEL
CHAPTER NINE

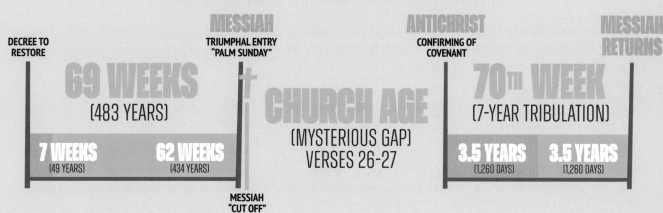

MESSIAH
TRIUMPHAL ENTRY
"PALM SUNDAY"

ANTICHRIST
CONFIRMING OF
COVENANT

**MESSIAH
RETURNS**

DECREE TO
RESTORE

69 WEEKS
(483 YEARS)

CHURCH AGE
(MYSTERIOUS GAP)
VERSES 26-27

70TH WEEK
(7-YEAR TRIBULATION)

7 WEEKS
(49 YEARS)

62 WEEKS
(434 YEARS)

3.5 YEARS
(1,260 DAYS)

3.5 YEARS
(1,260 DAYS)

MESSIAH
"CUT OFF"

WHO IS THE ANTICHRIST?

the little horn	**Daniel 7:8**
"a fierce-looking king"	**Daniel 8:23**
"a master of intrigue"	**Daniel 8:23**
"the ruler who will come"	**Daniel 9:26**
"a contemptible person"	**Daniel 11:21**
"a shepherd...who will not care"	**Zechariah 11:16**
"the worthless shepherd"	**Zechariah 11:16-17**
"man of lawlessness"	**2 Thessalonians 2:3**
"the lawless one"	**2 Thessalonians 2:8-9**
the rider on the white horse	**Revelation 6:2**
"a beast"	**Revelation 13:1**

THE BABYLONIAN EMPIRE

● JERUSALEM   ● BABYLON

THE MINOR PROPHETS

In the Old Testament are 12 books by the minor prophets, which were written over a span of 300 hundred years, from 760–460 BC. The Hebrew Bible unites these prophets into one book titled "the Book of the Twelve." Though this group of prophetic books is called minor, they are no less inspired or significant than the books by the major prophets (Isaiah, Jeremiah, Ezekiel, and Daniel). The main difference between the two groups is the length of their books. The minor prophets' messages are short yet powerful, and were written to Israel, Judah, or the surrounding nations.

	HOSEA	JOEL	AMOS	OBADIAH	JONAH	MICAH
Meaning of the Name	Salvation	Yahweh is God	Burden-bearer	Servant of the Lord	Dove	Who is like Yahweh?
Date	753–722 BC	9th–4th centuries BC	760 BC	586 BC	760 BC	742 BC
King	Zechariah	Unknown	Jeroboam II	Zedekiah	Jeroboam II	Jotham, Ahaz, Hezekiah
Recipient	Israel	Judah	Israel	Edom	Nineveh	Israel/Judah
Message	Judgment	Judgment	Judgment	Prophecy	Repentance	Judgment/ forgiveness
Purpose	Spiritual adultery	Repentance	Injustice	Against Edom	Show mercy	Discipline/ restore
Outline	Command to marry an unfaithful wife (1–3) Warnings and promises to an unfaithful nation (4–14)	Judgment and the day of the Lord (1–2) Mercy and judgment against the nations (2–3)	Judgments on Israel and neighbors (1–6) Visions of judgment (7–9)	Prophecy of Edom's judgment (verses 1-9) Indictment of Edom (verses 10-14) Israel is victorious (verses 15-21)	Jonah's flight from God (1) Jonah's prayer (2) Jonah's message (3) Jonah's anger (4)	Message of judgment and deliverance (1–5) Lord's indictment and restoration of his people (6–7)
Christological Theme	Only Savior, Son of God, one who ransoms from the dead, and Bridegroom	Baptizer with the Holy Spirit	Bearer of our sins	Mighty Savior	Forgiving Savior	The Everlasting One
Key Verses	4:6; 11:1; 13:4	2:28	5:14	10	1:17 (cf. Matthew 12:40); 4:2	6:8

JONAH: THE STORY

The book of Jonah tells the story of the prophet's rocky relationship with God and the lessons he learned along the way. The following events ultimately led to Jonah's obedience, and God's will was fulfilled.

- God calls Jonah to preach to the Ninevites, who were the exceedingly wicked and cruel enemies of God's people. Jonah must have viewed this as a suicide mission (1:1-2).
- Jonah flees from God to Joppa, then boards a ship for bound for Tarshish (1:3).
- God causes a great storm to threaten the ship and the lives of the sailors (1:4-6).
- After the sailors cast lots to discover what had caused the terrible storm, Jonah confesses that he has been fleeing from the Lord (1:7-11).
- Jonah tells the sailors to throw him overboard so the storm will cease. They throw him overboard, and the sea becomes calm (1:12-16).
- God prepares a big fish to swallow Jonah to save him from drowning (1:17).
- For three days, Jonah prays and calls upon the Lord while in the belly of the fish. On the third day, the fish releases Jonah on dry land (2:1, 10).
- God again commands Jonah to go to Nineveh and preach a message of coming destruction (3:1-3).
- After entering the city, Jonah declares that message: "Yet forty days, and Nineveh shall be overthrown!" (3:4).
- Jonah's message has a positive effect on the people and the king, and they repent. As a result, the Lord does not destroy Nineveh (3:6-10).
- Jonah becomes angry because it looks as though he was lying to the Ninevites and God didn't keep his word (4:1-4).
- Jonah builds a structure for shade, and God causes a plant to grow in order to give shade to Jonah. But soon after, God causes a worm to kill the plant, and the hot sun and harsh wind bring discomfort to Jonah (4:5-7).
- Jonah complains to God about the withered plant, and he feels justified in doing so (4:8-9).
- God challenges Jonah's priorities, telling the prophet that he is more concerned and indignant about the plant dying than about the 120,000 Ninevites who would have died had they not repented (4:10-11).

LIFE LESSONS FROM JONAH

- Life goes better for us when we obey God's Word and commands.
- Trust God even when you don't understand what is happening.
- Pray and call out to the Lord even when circumstances seem hopeless to you.
- Be sure to love others, including those who are difficult to love.
- Check your priorities and make sure they are in line with God's priorities.
- God is merciful.

THE MINOR PROPHETS

	NAHUM	HABAKKUK	ZEPHANIAH	HAGGAI	ZECHARIAH	MALACHI
Meaning of the name	Consolation	Embracer	The Lord hides	My feast	Yahweh remembers	My messenger
Date	660–630 BC	640–597 BC	640–628 BC	520 BC	520 BC	430–400 BC
King	Manasseh	Josiah	Josiah	Darius I	Darius I	Artaxerxes I/ Darius II
Recipient	Judah/ Nineveh	Judah	Judah	Judah	Judah	Judah
Message	Judgment	Judgment	Repentance from pagan worship	Exhortation	Hope	Indictment against Israel
Purpose	Rebuke Assyria's cruel and violent ways	Addresses Judah's spiritual deterioration	To inform of the consequences of the day of the Lord	Encourage God's people to complete the temple	Give hope to the remnant through reminders and prophecies of the coming Messiah	Spiritual apathy
Outline	Judgment and encouraging hope for Judah (1) Destruction of Nineveh (2–3)	Habakkuk and God in dialogue (1–2) Habakkuk prays and trusts (3)	Judgment on Judah and the nations (1–2) Judah's restoration (3)	Rebuilding the temple (1) Repentance, blessings, and David's throne (2)	Oracles and visions (1–8) Return of the Messiah (King) (9–14)	Identification of sin (1–3) Reward for the righteous (4)
Christological Theme	The jealous avenger of God's people	The holy God	The restorer	Cleanser of sins	The crucified Messiah	Sun of righteousness will rise with healing in its wings
Key Verses	1:2, 7	1:12-13; 3:18	1:14	2:5	9:9	4:2

THE MESSAGE OF ZECHARIAH

VISION 1

Horseman who patrols the earth (1:7-17)

The Lord will rebuild his house, forgive his people, and restore them to prosperity.

VISION 2

Four horns and the four craftsmen (1:18-21)

The Lord will cast down the nations who scattered and oppressed his people.

VISION 3

Man with a measuring line comes to measure Jerusalem (2:1-13)

Jerusalem will be inhabited, and the Lord will protect and dwell in the midst of his people.

VISION 4

Joshua the high priest has his filthy clothes cleaned (3:1-10)

God will cleanse the nation of unrighteousness and offer forgiveness. Joshua will rule the Lord's house and the coming of the Messiah ("the Branch") is promised.

VISION 5

The golden lampstand, bowl, and lamps with two olive trees (4:1-14)

The rebuilding of the temple will occur by the hands of Zerubbabel and Joshua through God's power.

VISION 6

The flying scroll (5:1-4)

The curses of the covenant will come upon those who break the covenant.

VISION 7

Woman in the basket carried away by two women (5:5-11)

The wickedness of God's people will be carried away into exile to the land of Shinar, where it will reside.

VISION 8

Four chariots pulled by four horses that are red, black, white, and gray (dappled) (6:1-8)

The four horses and chariots patrol the earth from north to south, executing the Lord's divine judgment ("mountains of bronze") and rule ("set my Spirit at rest").

ZECHARIAH

THE INTERTESTAMENTAL SILENT YEARS

The 400-year period of time between the completion of the Old Testament (ca. 430–400 BC) and the coming of Christ is known as the intertestamental period, or the silent years, when there was no prophetic voice to speak to God's people. By the end of the prophet Malachi's ministry, the nation had already returned from its exile in Babylon and rebuilt the temple as well as the walls and Jerusalem's infrastructure. Israel only lacked one thing: a king. In the fullness of time, God sent his Son (Galatians 4:4) to Israel as their King and long-awaited Messiah of whom the prophets foretold. But before Christ arrived, God was busy preparing the world in various ways to receive Jesus. Among them was uniting the world under a universal language (Greek), a sound judicial and political system, a formidable military to keep the peace, physical infrastructure such as roads, and the ability to worship freely as long as the population remained peaceful. These important preparations took place during the silent years, which came to an end prior to Jesus' birth in Bethlehem as the King of the Jews.

INTERTESTAMENTAL TIMELINE

MALACHI

ALEXANDER THE GREAT

JUDAS MACCABEUS

ANTIOCHUS IV

400 BC — The last book of the Old Testament is written, the book of Malachi.

332 BC — The Persians (Darius III) fall to Alexander the Great (Greece).

331–164 BC — The Hellenistic period is marked by the spread of Greek culture and language throughout the world (Hellenism).

323 BC — Alexander the Great dies and his empire is divided into four regions to be ruled by his four generals (Lysimachus, Cassander, Ptolemy, Seleucus).

320–198 BC — The Ptolemaic region rules over the Jews while Greek culture continues to spread.

250 BC — The Hebrew Scriptures are translated into the Greek language to accommodate the growing number of Greek-speaking Jews in Egypt. The translation is called the Septuagint (LXX) and would become the Bible of Jesus and his disciples.

198 BC — The Seleucid Empire begins ruling the Jews and implements strict policies forbidding many of the practices of Judaism, thus transforming the temple into a pagan shrine.

198–164 BC — The Seleucids persecute Israel until a priest named Mattathias, along with his five sons (including Judas Maccabeus), wins the nation's independence through the Maccabean Revolt.

168 BC — Seleucid ruler Antiochus IV Epiphanes (reigned 175–164 BC) desecrates the Jerusalem temple by looting it and erecting an idol devoted to Zeus (Jupiter). Later, Antiochus sacrifices swine on the altar.

164 BC—Jerusalem and the temple are reclaimed by the Maccabean Revolt. The temple is cleansed and the daily sacrifices resume. This event is commemorated by Hanukkah (the Festival of Lights) every November/December.

164–63 BC—Israel is ruled by the Maccabean family, and this era is known as the Hasmonean period. Hasmonean rule deteriorated to such an extent that the Roman general Pompey was invited to restore order.

PHARISEES/SADDUCEES

152–142 BC—The Sadducees, Pharisees, and Essenes are mentioned for the first time as flourishing during the high priesthood of Jonathan (cf. Josephus, *Jewish Antiquities* 13.171).

64 BC—Syria becomes a Roman province, which expands Roman rule into Palestine.

64 BC–AD 180—During the Early Roman period, Pompey comes to Jerusalem and restores order and brings Roman rule with him.

63 BC—Pompey enters the Jewish temple and offends the Jews. This is the beginning of ever-worsening relations with Rome, which would lead to a Jewish rebellion and the destruction of the temple in AD 70.

POMPEY

37 BC—Herod is appointed king of all Palestine and is reigning at the time Jesus was born in Bethlehem in ca. 5–4 BC.

31 BC—Caesar Augustus becomes emperor of the Roman Empire.

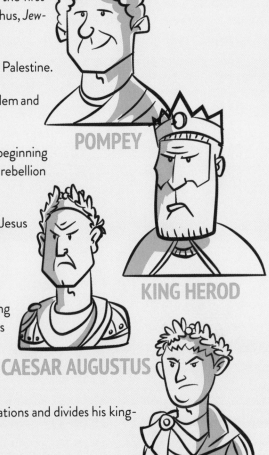

20 BC—Herod begins remodeling the Temple Mount and its surrounding infrastructure (retaining walls). This rebuilding program continues beyond his death until AD 64.

KING HEROD

5–4 BC—Jesus is born in Bethlehem.

4 BC—Herod the Great dies before completing the Temple Mount renovations and divides his kingdom between his three sons—Archelaus, Philip, and Antipas.

4 BC—Herod Archelaus rules Judea, Samaria, and Idumea until he is banished in AD 6. He is replaced by various governors until Pontius Pilate became prefect of the territory. Herod Philip rules the area northeast of Galilee until his death in AD 34. Herod Antipas reigns over Galilee and Perea until his death in AD 39.

CAESAR AUGUSTUS

AD 14—Tiberius becomes Roman emperor and reigns until AD 37.

TIBERIUS CAESAR

AD 26–36—Pontius Pilate is established as governor of Judea after earlier mismanagement by Herod Archelaus.

CA. AD 26–28—Jesus is crucified under Pilate and the Roman emperor Tiberius.

AD 40–100—The New Testament is written.

PONTIUS PILATE

5/4 BC — Birth of Christ in Bethlehem

4 BC — Joseph, Mary, and Jesus flee to Egypt to avoid persecution by Herod; they return after Herod's death (Matthew 2:13-18)

AD 9 — At age 12, Jesus speaks with the teachers in the temple (Luke 2:41-50)

AD 8–26 — Jesus lives in Nazareth and works as a carpenter (Matthew 13:55; Mark 6:3)

AD 27–29 — Jesus begins his ministry at 30 years of age (Luke 3:23)

AD 28/29 — John the Baptist baptizes in the Jordan (John 1:19)

AD 30 — Jesus is beaten, tried, and crucified on Golgotha and buried (Matthew 26–27)

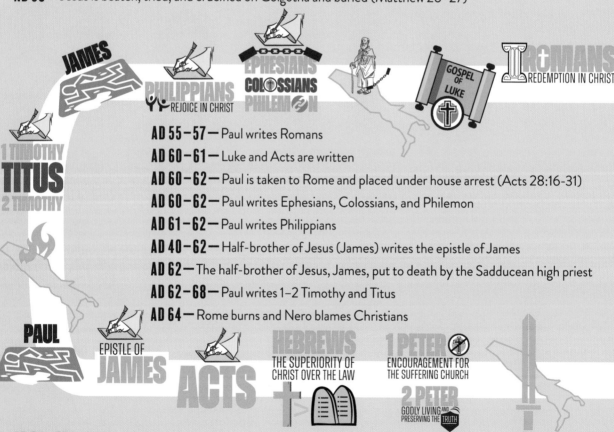

AD 55–57 — Paul writes Romans

AD 60–61 — Luke and Acts are written

AD 60–62 — Paul is taken to Rome and placed under house arrest (Acts 28:16-31)

AD 60–62 — Paul writes Ephesians, Colossians, and Philemon

AD 61–62 — Paul writes Philippians

AD 40–62 — Half-brother of Jesus (James) writes the epistle of James

AD 62 — The half-brother of Jesus, James, put to death by the Sadducean high priest

AD 62–68 — Paul writes 1–2 Timothy and Titus

AD 64 — Rome burns and Nero blames Christians

AD 64–67 — Paul is executed

AD 60–70 — Book of Hebrews is written

AD 65–69 — Peter writes 1–2 Peter

AD 66 — Jewish war against Rome begins

Unlike the Old Testament, which was written over a period of 1,100 years, the New Testament was written within a 60-year span of time. The four Gospels provide portraits of Jesus' life and ministry. The book of Acts offers a glimpse into how the gospel spread around the world. The Epistles teach the doctrines of the Christian faith and their applications to life. And the book of Revelation foretells end-time events and the consummation of all things in Christ.

AD 30 — Jesus rises from the dead three days after his crucifixion (Matthew 28)

AD 30 — Jesus appears to many for 40 days (Acts 1:3)

AD 30–34 — Stephen is stoned to death (Acts 7)

AD 34–37 — Paul sees Jesus on the road to Damascus and goes to Arabia (Acts 9:1-9; Galatians 1:15-16)

AD 46–47 — Paul's first missionary journey to Asia Minor, with Barnabas (Acts 13–14)

AD 48–49 — Paul writes Galatians

AD 49 — Claudius bans Jews from Rome (Acts 18:2-3)

AD 49–51 — Paul's second missionary journey, this time including Europe, with Silas; Paul writes 1–2 Thessalonians (Acts 15–18)

 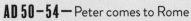    

AD 50–54 — Peter comes to Rome

AD 50–55 — Gospel of Matthew is written

AD 50–63 — Gospel of Mark is written

AD 50S–70S — Half-brother of Jesus, Jude, writes the epistle of Jude

AD 52–57 — Paul's third missionary journey, to Asia Minor and Greece (Acts 18–21)

AD 52–55 — Paul ministers in Ephesus

AD 55–56 — Paul writes 1–2 Corinthians

AD 70 — Romans destroy Jerusalem and the temple

AD 85–95 — John writes the Gospel of John and 1, 2, and 3 John from Ephesus

AD 93–94 — Josephus writes *Jewish Histories* from Rome

AD 94–95 — Book of Revelation written by John on island of Patmos

MATTHEW: THE PROMISED MESSIAH

The first book of the New Testament was written to Jews by a former Jewish tax-collector, Matthew, an apostle of Jesus (Matthew 10:1-3). As the first of three synoptic (meaning "from the same point of view") Gospels, Matthew emphasized Jesus as the fulfillment of the Old Testament promise of a Messiah to the Jews as well as the establishing of God's kingdom. He refers to Old Testament books about 130 times and presents Christ's ancestry in order to demonstrate that Christ is the King of the Jews.

QUICK FACTS

Date: AD 50–55
Theme: Christ is the Messiah and King of the Jews
Recipients: Jews in Syria
Ancestry: Descended from Abraham and David
Literature: Long discourses, historical narrative, nine beatitudes, and 45 parables

KEY WORDS: *Fulfilled* and *fulfill* used 15 times of Christ, *end of the age, Father, kingdom, kingdom of heaven, righteousness, son of David, worship, which was spoken* (in the Old Testament)

KEY VERSE: "Say to the daughter of Zion, 'Behold, your king is coming to you, humble, and mounted on a donkey, on a colt, the foal of a beast of burden'" (Matthew 21:5).

OUTLINE

MESSIAH
מָשִׁיחַ

1. The person of the Messiah (1–3)
2. The preparation of the Messiah (4)
3. The proclamation of the Messiah (5–9)
4. The propagation of the Messiah (10–25)
5. The suffering of the Messiah (26–27)
6. The power of the Messiah (28)

ANCESTRY OF JESUS THROUGH JOSEPH

Unlike the Gospel of Luke, which traces Mary's *physical* ancestry, Matthew offers Jesus' *legal* ancestry through Joseph, his legal adoptive father, which establishes Christ's legal authority to sit on the throne of David (Matthew 1:1-16).

ABRAHAM	JOTHAM
ISAAC	AHAZ
JACOB	HEZEKIAH
JUDAH	MANASSEH
PEREZ	AMOS
HEZRON	JOSIAH
RAM	JECONIAH
AMMINADAB	SHEALTIEL
NAHSHON	ZERUBBABEL
SALMON	ABIUD
BOAZ	ELIAKIM
OBED	AZOR
JESSE	ZADOK
DAVID	ACHIM
SOLOMON	ELIUD
REHOBOAM	ELEAZAR
ABIJAH	MATTHAN
ASAPH	JACOB
JEHOSHAPHAT	JOSEPH (LEGAL FATHER OF JESUS)
JORAM	
UZZIAH	JESUS

KEY PARABLES
IN MATTHEW

The two foundations (7:24-27): In contrast to other options, the words of Christ provide the most stable foundation for us to build on.

The new cloth and wineskins (9:16-17): Christ's teachings are like new wine placed in new wineskins, not a patch repair made to the old cloth of the Judaic system.

The sower (13:1-8): Different people show varying levels of responsiveness to God's Word.

The weeds (13:24-30): The wicked and the good will exist together until Christ's kingdom comes.

The mustard seed (13:31-32): The kingdom of heaven will start small and will grow large over time.

The yeast (13:33): The kingdom of heaven will have a pervasive influence and spread throughout the earth.

JESUS

The treasure (13:44): The kingdom of heaven has great worth.

The pearl of great price (13:45-46): Total commitment to the kingdom of heaven is warranted due to its great worth.

The dragnet (13:47-50): The wicked and the good will coexist until they are separated at the arrival of Christ's kingdom.

The householder (13:52): We have the ability to learn from Christ's parables.

The lost sheep (18:12-14): This speaks to everyone's need to repent of sin.

The unmerciful servant (18:23-35): We need to be like God and freely forgive others.

The workers in the vineyard (20:1-16): God offers generous grace for everyone.

The two sons (21:28-32): The immoral person who repents will enter the kingdom, but not the unrepentant "moral" person.

The tenants (21:33-46): God removes stewardship from the unfaithful and entrusts it to those who are faithful.

The wedding banquet (22:1-14): God invites all to his kingdom, but only the repentant will be blessed.

The wise and wicked servants (24:45-51): True followers of Jesus will be watching and preparing for his return.

Ten virgins (25:1-13): This is a call to be prepared for Christ's imminent return.

Talents (25:14-30): This is another call to prepare for the coming of Christ.

GOSPEL OF MARK: GOD'S RIGHTEOUS SERVANT

MARK

Mark was an associate of Peter (1 Peter 5:13) and accompanied Paul on one of his missionary journeys (Acts 13:5). He was also a relative of Barnabas (Colossians 4:10). The book portrays Christ as a *servant* to a Roman-reading audience. Mark recognized the need to give an answer to people who wondered why they should receive Christ when his own people, the Jews, rejected him. His explanation of the gospel is *active* and focuses on what Jesus *does* rather than what he *says*.

QUICK FACTS

Date: AD 50–63
Location: Readers of Mark were in Rome
Theme: Christ as the servant of God
Unique Aspect: No ancestry is presented because servants are humble and, in that context, pedigree is not important

OUTLINE

1. The ministry of the Servant (1–8)
2. The offering of the Servant (9–15)
3. The glory of the Servant (16)

KEY WORDS: *Immediately* (40 times), *straightway*, *authority*, and *Spirit*

KEY VERSE: "The Son of Man came not to be served but to serve, and to give his life as a ransom for many" (Mark 10:45).

THE TWELVE APOSTLES

Though Mark was not an apostle (Mark 3:14-19), the Bible tells us about the 12 men Jesus chose to serve alongside him (Matthew 10:2-4). After the death and resurrection of Christ, the message of the gospel was spread by the apostles in Jerusalem, Judea, Samaria, and then around the world (Acts 1:8). Because little is known about the apostles' subsequent ministries and deaths, we rely on early church sources to provide more information about each of them.

THE SERVANT'S CRUCIFIXION TIME LINE

- Jesus is taken to Golgotha, the place of the skull (15:22)
- He refuses to drink the wine mixed with myrrh (verse 23)
- Soldiers gamble for his one-piece garment (verse 24)
- Jesus is crucified at 9:00 am (verses 24-28)
- "King of the Jews" sign is placed on the cross (verse 26)
- Thieves who were crucified alongside Christ revile him (verse 32)
- Darkness covers the area at noon (verses 33)
- Jesus cries in agony, "My God, My God, why have you forsaken me?" (verse 34)
- Jesus receives sour wine (verse 36)
- Jesus dismisses his spirit and dies at 3:00 pm (verse 37)
- The earth shakes and the temple curtain is torn in two (verse 38)
- Soldiers acknowledge Jesus is the Son of God (verse 39)
- Jesus is buried in Joseph of Arimathea's tomb prior to sunset (verses 42-46)

THE APOSTLES

Apostle	Identity	Hometown	Character	Profession	Relation to Others	Region of Ministry	Death
Peter	Son of Jonah/ Cephas (rock/ stone)	Bethsaida	Impetuous	Fisherman	Brother of Andrew/ friend of Mark	Rome	Martyr
James	Son of Zebedee/sons of thunder	Galilee	Fiery	Fisherman	Brother of John	Spain	Martyr
John	Son of Zebedee/sons of thunder	Galilee	Fiery	Fisherman	Brother of James	Ephesus (Turkey)	Died of natural causes
Andrew	The first called by Jesus	Bethsaida	Spiritual seeker	Fisherman	Brother of Peter	Greece, Turkey, Russia	Martyr
Philip	Name means "lover of horses"	Bethsaida	Practical/seeking understanding	Unknown/ Greek background	He is not Philip the evangelist in Acts	Scythia (Ukraine)	Martyr
Bartholomew	Nathaniel	Cana	Honest/ sincere	Unknown	Friend	Turkey, India	Martyr
Matthew	The tax collector	Galilee	Humble	Tax collector	Maybe brother to James, son of Alphaeus	Persia, Macedonia, Ethiopia	Martyr
Thomas	The Didymus (twin)	Unknown	Doubter	Unknown	Friend	India	Martyr
James	Son of Alphaeus/James the Younger	Unknown	Zealot	Unknown	Possibly brother to Matthew/not James the half brother of Jesus	Jerusalem	Martyr
Thaddaeus	Son of James/ Labbaeus/ Jude	Unknown	Seeking understanding	Unknown	Friend/not Jude the half brother of Jesus	Unknown	Unknown
Simon	The zealot	Unknown	Patriot	Insurrectionist	Friend	Persia	Unknown
Judas	Son of Simon	Near Kerioth in Judea	Greedy/ betrayer	Treasurer	Friend/ replaced by Matthias	None	Suicide

GOSPEL OF LUKE: SAVIOR FOR THE GENTILES

The third Gospel was written by Luke (who was not an apostle) to a cultured Greek convert to Christianity named Theophilus, whose name means "lover of God" (1:3). Luke is believed to have been a physician by trade (Colossians 4:14), as evidenced by the medical vocabulary he uses throughout this Gospel. He was also a traveling companion of Paul (2 Timothy 4:11) and most likely a Gentile due to his absence from the list of circumcised brethren in Colossians 4:10-14. Shortly after completing this Gospel, he also wrote the book of Acts, which is a sequel to Luke. After consulting eyewitnesses (1:2), Luke presented Christ as a Savior for the Gentiles, tracing his ancestry back to Adam while, at the same time, demonstrating that Christ was a descendant from the bloodline of King David through Mary's genealogy.

LUKE

QUICK FACTS

Date: AD 59–60
Author: Luke the physician
Theme: The Son of Man is the Savior for the Gentiles
Recipient: Theophilus (1:3) and the Gentile world
Location: Readers may have been in Caesarea (Acts 23:23-24)

OUTLINE

1. The humanity of the Son of Man (1–4)
2. The activity of the Son of Man (5–23)
3. The majesty of the Son of Man (24)

KEY WORDS: *Save* and *Savior* (21 times), *sin and sinner* (18 times), *salvation, preach the good news, grace*

KEY VERSE: "The Son of Man has come to seek and to save that which was lost" (Luke 19:10).

REIGNS OF ROMAN EMPERORS DURING THE NEW TESTAMENT

AUGUSTUS	27 BC–AD 14:	Jesus born (2:1)
TIBERIUS	AD 14–37:	Jesus crucified (3:1)
CALIGULA	AD 37–41	
CLAUDIUS	AD 41–54:	Severe famine (Acts 11:28); expelled Jews from Rome (Acts 18:2)
NERO	AD 54–68:	Paul and Peter martyred
GALBA	AD 68	
OTHO	AD 69	
VITELLIUS	AD 69	
VESPASIAN	AD 69–79:	Defeated the Jewish revolt that began in AD 66
TITUS	AD 79–81:	Destroyed Jerusalem and the temple in AD 70
DOMITIAN	AD 81–96:	Persecutor of Christians
NERVA	AD 96–98	
TRAJAN	AD 98–117	

ANCESTRY OF JESUS THROUGH MARY

Unlike the Gospel of Matthew, which traces Joseph's ancestry, Luke offers Jesus' *physical* ancestry through Mary, his biological mother, which establishes Christ's physical authority to sit on the throne of David (Luke 3:23-38). Whereas Joseph descended from David through his son Solomon, which gives Jesus the *legal* right to claim the throne of David, Mary descended from David through his son Nathan, giving Jesus the physical (bloodline) right to claim the Davidic throne.

ADAM	TERAH	ELIAKIM	JOANAN
SETH	ABRAHAM	JONAM	JODA
ENOS	ISAAC	JOSEPH	JOSECH
CAINAN	JACOB	JUDAH	SEMEIN
MAHALALEEL	JUDAH	SIMEON	MATTATHIAS
JARED	PEREZ	LEVI	MAATH
ENOCH	HEZRON	MATTHAT	NAGGAI
METHUSELAH	ARNI (AKA RAM OR ARAM)	JORIM	ESLI
LAMECH	ADMIN (AMMINADAB)	ELIEZER	NAHUM
NOAH	NAHSHON	JOSHUA	AMOS
SHEM	SALA (SALMON)	ER	MATTATHIAS
ARPHAXAD	BOAZ	ELMADAM	JOSEPH
CAINAN	OBED	COSAM	JANNAI
SHELAH	JESSE	ADDI	MELCHI
EBER	DAVID	MELCHI	LEVI
PELEG	NATHAN	NERI	MATTHAT
REU	MATTATHA	SHEALTIEL	HELI
SERUG	MENNA	ZERUBBABEL	JOSEPH THE LEGAL FATHER (MARY THE BIRTH MOTHER)
NAHOR	MELEA	RHESA	JESUS

JOHN: THE DIVINE SAVIOR OF THE WORLD

Though the book's title is "The Gospel According to John," nowhere in the Gospel does the apostle John explicitly identify himself as the writer. A few decades after the book was written, early Christians applied the title to distinguish it from earlier accounts of the life of Christ written by Matthew, Mark, and Luke (known as the Synoptic Gospels, meaning "from the same point of view"). John's Gospel is distinguished from the Synoptics due to the high amount of unique content in it. John presents Jesus as God in human flesh, developing the Gospel like an orchestra building to a crescendo. He starts with the lowly and humble message of the incarnation (1:1, 14—God takes on a human nature) and then builds through a series of eight miracles, eight witnesses, and eight Christocentric "I am" statements, to an apex culminating in Thomas's realization that Jesus is "My Lord and my God!" (20:28).

JOHN

JOHN AS THE AUTHOR

Despite John's anonymity and five veiled allusions of himself within the book as "one of his disciples, whom Jesus loved" (13:23; see also 19:26; 20:2; 21:7, 20), his authorship is well attested externally by the early church fathers. Though there are early citations of the Gospel by Tatian (a student of Justin Martyr) and Apollinaris (the bishop of Heiropolis), Theophilus of Antioch (who died AD 180) was the first to cite John as the author. What's more, the fourth-century church historian Eusebius tells us that two second-century theologians, Clement of Alexandria and Tertullian, widely attest to John as the author. In addition, before Ireneus's death in AD 202, he relates the personal conversations he had as a young boy with John's disciple, Polycarp (the bishop of Smyrna), who affirmed John's authorship prior to his death in AD 156. By the end of the second century, only a couple of fringe groups (such as the Alogoi) rejected Johannine authorship.

QUICK FACTS

Includes 92 percent unique content not found in the other Gospels
Written ca. AD 85–95
Written in Ephesus

PURPOSE for WRITING

John states his twofold purpose for writing the Gospel that emphasizes the words *believe* (Greek *pisteuo*, used 98 times in the book) and *life* (Greek *zoe*, used 36 times) (20:30-31). The Gospel offers a portrait of the Messiah that (1) seeks to lead the reader to *believe* that Jesus is the Christ, the Son of God, and (2) says you can have *life* by believing in his name.

KEY VERSE: "I came that they may have life and have it abundantly" (John 10:10).

OUTLINE

1. The prologue (1:1-18)
2. The public ministry of Christ (1:19–12:50)
3. The private ministry of Christ (13–17)
4. The passion (suffering) of Christ (18–19)
5. The resurrection of Christ (20)
6. The epilogue (21)

THE RESURRECTED LORD

After Jesus was in the tomb of Joseph of Arimathea for three days, he fulfilled prophecy (Psalm 16:10; Matthew 12:40; Luke 9:22) and rose physically from the grave. During the next 40 days, he demonstrated to others that he was alive, showing himself to many on various occasions.

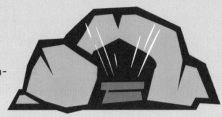

Importance of the Resurrection (1 Corinthians 15:12-19)

Without the resurrection...

- our preaching is in vain
- our faith is in vain
- we are false witnesses of the resurrection
- our faith is worthless
- we are still in our sins
- those who have died have no hope of life
- we are to be pitied

Theological Importance of the Resurrection

- The resurrection is the heart of the gospel
- It proves Jesus is the Son of God
- It gives believers a living hope
- It separates Jesus from other religious figures
- It is a picture of the Christian life—born again into a new life
- Christ's resurrection body sets the precedent that we, too, will have resurrected bodies

Twelve Facts All Scholars (Conservative and Liberal) Believe About the Resurrection

1. Jesus died by crucifixion
2. He was buried
3. After his death, the disciples despaired and lost hope
4. Tomb was discovered empty
5. Disciples experienced what they thought was the resurrected Christ
6. Disciples were transformed from doubters to bold proclaimers
7. The resurrection was the center of the spoken gospel message
8. The message was proclaimed in Jerusalem shortly after Jesus died
9. The church was born as a result of the spoken gospel message
10. Sunday became the primary day of worship
11. James, who was a skeptic, was converted when he said he saw the risen Christ
12. Paul was converted when he said he saw the risen Christ

Positive Evidence for the Resurrected Jesus

- More than 500 eyewitnesses of the resurrected Jesus
- The empty tomb
- Changed lives of the disciples
- Earliest records describe the resurrection as fact
- Lack of early records refuting the resurrection
- The divergent perspectives and independence of the writers argue in favor of credible history
- Credible assessment of the records by authorities in history and law (C.J. Hemer, A.N. Sherwin-White, Simon Greenleaf)
- The presence of counterproductive features, such as Jesus appearing to women first and revealing the flaws of the disciples (e.g., Peter's denial of Jesus), which indicate credible history

JESUS' FINAL HOURS

THURSDAY	FRIDAY	SATURDAY	SUNDAY
NISAN 14	**NISAN 15**	**NISAN 16**	**NISAN 17**
The day of preparation for Passover week (Feast of Unleavened Bread) lasts until Friday at sunset (John 19:14; cf. verse 31).	Day 1 in the tomb	Day 2 in the tomb	Day 3 in the tomb; Jesus rises on the third day
Thursday is the day of preparation prior to Passover week, which started at sunset (John 19:14). Passover begins at sunset and initiates the 7-day Feast of Unleavened Bread. Jesus eats his final Passover dinner with disciples. Judas leaves the meal to betray Jesus.	In the early morning hours, Jesus is whipped and beaten. Pilate completes the trials with Jesus' sentence of death, despite announcing earlier that he had found no fault in Jesus.	Jesus' body remains in the tomb on the Sabbath.	Jesus is in the tomb in the early morning hours.
Jesus leaves with his disciples to pray at the garden of Gethsemane. Later that night, Judas leads the temple guards to Gethsemane and Jesus is arrested.	Jesus is led away to Golgotha, outside the city, to be crucified at 9:00 am (Mark 15:25). Darkness covers the land at about noon (Mark 15:33).	Jesus remains in the tomb.	Jesus is risen from the dead and comes out of the tomb early Sunday morning while it's still dark.
The Jews begin their interrogation of Jesus and commence 6 trials through the night and early morning by Annas, Caiaphas, the Sanhedrin, Pontius Pilate, Herod, and back to Pilate.	Jesus dies at 3:00 pm (Mark 15:34-37), fulfilling the timing of the lamb's death as being "between the two evenings" (i.e., twilight) (see Exodus 12:6). A severe earthquake ensues and tears the temple partition in half. Jesus is hurriedly buried in the tomb of Joseph of Arimathea prior to sunset (John 19:31, 42).	Jesus remains in the tomb past sunset into very early Sunday morning.	Angels at the tomb speak to Mary, who sees the risen Jesus and tells the disciples. Peter and John run to the tomb and see it empty with a folded head cloth. Jesus then makes multiple appearances over a period of 40 days to show he has risen, along with other convincing proofs.

THE DEITY OF CHRIST

The Bible teaches that Jesus is God. This is affirmed in numerous ways.

Affirmed by the Fulfillment of Prophecy Isaiah 53; cf. John 18–19

Micah 5:2; cf. Matthew 2:1
Psalm 16:10; cf. John 20

Affirmed by Biblical Testimony

Psalms 45:6-7; 110:1; Proverbs 30:4; Isaiah 9:6; John 1:1, 14; 8:58; 10:30; Colossians 1:15-17; Titus 2:13; 2 Peter 1:1

Affirmed by Jesus' Sinless and Miraculous Life

Luke 23:14-15, 47; Romans 1:4; 4:25; Hebrews 4:15; 1 Peter 1:18-19

THE CRUCIFIXION FULFILLS THE PASSOVER

PASSOVER	CRUCIFIXION OF THE LAMB OF GOD
The lamb must be of the first year (Exodus 11:47; 12:5; 12:29-30)	Jesus was the firstborn of Mary and of God (Colossians 1:15)
The lamb must be a male from the flock (Exodus 12:5)	Jesus was born a man like his brethren (Romans 5:12-21; 1 Corinthians 15:22)
The lamb must be without spot or blemish (Exodus 12:5)	Jesus had no sin, no inherent or acquired defect (Hebrews 4:15; 1 Peter 1:18-20)
The lamb must be inspected for imperfections (Exodus 12:5)	Jesus was inspected through 6 trials and by the thief on the cross (Matthew 27:4; John 18:38)
The lamb must be killed between the two evenings of Nisan 14 sunset (Thursday) and Nisan 15 sunset (Friday) (Exodus 12:6)	Jesus was crucified between Nisan 14 sunset and Nisan 15 sunset (Mark 15:33)
The lamb must be killed by the whole assembly (Exodus 12:6)	Jesus was killed by the Sanhedrin, the priests, and the Jewish people who called for his death (John 19:15)
The lamb's blood must be applied to the doorposts to save the household (Exodus 12:7, 13, 22)	Jesus' blood must be applied and is the only way to salvation (Matthew 26:26-28; Acts 20:28; Hebrews 9:14)
The lamb must be eaten (Exodus 12:8-10)	Jesus ate the Passover meal with his disciples and offered the bread (figurative of his body) and the cup (figurative of his blood) to be eaten. His sacrifice must be remembered through the ordinance of communion (Luke 22:19-20; John 6:53; 1 Corinthians 11:23-25)
The lamb's bones were not to be broken (Exodus 12:46; Psalm 34:20)	Jesus was already deceased, so his legs were not broken (John 19:33-37)
Passover is to be a memorial (Exodus 12:14)	Jesus instituted the Lord's supper as a memorial (Matthew 26:26-28)
Passover is to be accompanied by 7 days of unleavened bread (Exodus 12:15-20, 34, 39)	Jesus calls everyone to repent and be separated from sin (John 8:34-36)

Affirmed by His Being Worshipped as God on Numerous Occasions

Healed leper worships Jesus (Matthew 8:2)
Ruler kneels before Jesus (Matthew 9:18)
Disciples worship Jesus (Matthew 14:33)
Mother of James and John worships Jesus (Matthew 20:20)
Thomas worships Jesus (John 20:28)
Angels worship Jesus (Hebrews 1:6)
Gerasene demoniac falls down before Jesus (Mark 5:6)
Disciples worship Jesus again (Matthew 28:16-17)
Blind man worships Jesus (John 9:38)
Canaanite woman worships before Jesus (Matthew 15:25)

Affirmed by the Fact He Shares These Titles with God

I AM	FORGIVER
SHEPHERD	LORD
CREATOR	OMNISCIENT
FIRST AND THE LAST	OMNIPRESENT
GOD	OMNIPOTENT
SAVIOR	UNCHANGING

ACTS: THE BIRTH AND GROWTH OF THE CHURCH

The book of Acts presents a fascinating overview of how the church grew from a small group of faithful believers in Jerusalem, then spread throughout Judea, Samaria, and to the ends of the earth (Acts 1:8). The Roman historian Tacitus wrote that the Christian faith reached all the way to Rome, the capital of the empire. The events documented in Acts cover a span of approximately 30 years from the ascension of Christ to Paul's house arrest in Rome, roughly AD 30–61. During this time, Paul had traveled extensively, conducting three missionary journeys through Asia Minor (Turkey) and Europe, and wrote the bulk of his 13 epistles. Acts was written by Luke around AD 61.

OUTLINE OF ACTS

PAUL

Author	Luke, the physician							
Years	AD 30–33			AD 34–45			AD 46–61	
Apostle	Peter and John			Peter and Philip			Paul	
Chapters	1–2	3–4	5	6–7	8–9	10–12	13	14
Location	Jerusalem			Judea and Samaria			Ends of the earth	
Emperor	Tiberius (AD 13–37)			Caligula (37–41)			Claudius (41–54)	
Epistles Written	None							
Key Verse(s)	1:8	4:12	5:12	6:7	9:31	10:15	13:2	14:21-22

Author	Luke, the physician							
Years	AD 46–61							
Apostle	Paul							
Chapters	15	16	17	18	19–20	21–23	24–26	27–28
Location	Ends of the earth							
Emperor	Claudius (41–54)				Nero (54–68)			
Epistles Written	James	Galatians	Thessalo-nians		Corinthians		Romans	Ephesians Philippians Colossians Philemon
Key Verse(s)	15:19-20	16:9	17:29	18:4	19:8	21:24	26:29	28:23

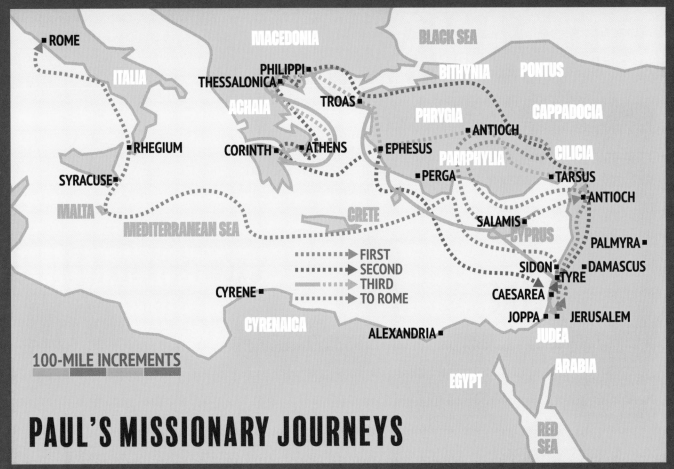

PAUL'S MISSIONARY JOURNEYS

The book of Acts documents three missionary journeys by Paul and his traveling companions. These journeys mark the earliest spread of the gospel message to destinations outside of Israel. Some received the message with gladness, while others rejected Paul's message and persecuted him and other Christians. Afterward, Paul was arrested in Jerusalem and taken to Rome to stand trial, where he was placed under house arrest for about two years. While in confinement from AD 60–61, Paul wrote the epistles of Colossians, Philippians, Ephesians, and Philemon.

FIRST MISSIONARY JOURNEY

Date: AD 47–49
Scripture: Acts 13–14
Travel Companions: Paul, Barnabas, Mark
Transportation: Ship and foot
Locations: Cyprus, Perga, Pisidian Antioch, Iconium, Lystra, Derbe, Lystra, Pisidian, Pamphylia, Perga, Attalia, Antioch
Distance: 1,400 miles

SECOND MISSIONARY JOURNEY

Date: AD 49–52
Scripture: Acts 15:36–18:22
Travel Companions: Two teams comprised of (1) Paul, Silas, Luke, and Timothy, and (2) Barnabas and Mark
Transportation: Ship and foot
Locations: Antioch, Syria, Celicia, Derbe, Lystra, Iconium, Phrygia, Galatia, Troas, Philippi, Thessalonica, Berea, Athens, Corinth, Ephesus, Caesarea, Antioch
Distance: 2,900 miles

THIRD MISSIONARY JOURNEY

Date: AD 52–56
Scripture: Acts 18:23–21:26
Travel Companions: Paul, Timothy, and Luke
Transportation: Ship and foot
Locations: Antioch, Galatia, Phrygia, Ephesus, Macedonia, Greece, Troas, Miletus, Ptolemias, Caesarea (Agabus prophesies that Paul will be arrested in Jerusalem), Jerusalem
Distance: 2,800 miles

TO ROME WHILE UNDER ARREST

Date: AD 57–61
Scripture: Acts 21:27–28:31
Travel Companions: Paul, Luke, and Roman guard
Transportation: Ship
Locations: Jerusalem, Caesarea, Sidon (Lebanon), Crete, Malta, Syracuse (Sicily), Rhegium, Puteoli, Appi Forum, Three Taverns, Rome
Distance: 2,300 miles

ROMANS: REDEMPTION IN CHRIST

In AD 56–57, while on his third missionary journey, Paul wrote the book of Romans to the believers in Rome (Romans 1:1; Acts 20:1-3). The importance of the epistle can't be overstated; it is a thorough explanation about redemption in Christ for all who believe (Romans 3:24). Paul addressed people's need to recognize their own sin and stated that faith in Christ is the only way to salvation. He also addressed God's sovereignty, judgment, human will, the church, the nation of Israel, and the believer's social, civic, and personal conduct.

OUTLINE

1. Doctrine of redemption (1–8)
2. Israel and redemption (9–11)
3. Christian duty and redemption (12–16)

KEY WORDS:

Believe, law, all (whole), Lord, Jesus Christ, faith, judgment, Spirit, salvation

KEY VERSE:
"I am not ashamed of the gospel, for it is the power of God for salvation to everyone who believes, to the Jew first and also to the Greek" (Romans 1:16).

NEW TESTAMENT KEY WORDS FOR REDEMPTION

AGORAZO
"to purchase or buy in the marketplace" (1 Corinthians 6:20)

EXAGORAZO
"to purchase out of the marketplace" (Galatians 3:13; 4:5)

LYTRON
"means of release, means of redeeming" (Matthew 20:28)

LYTROOMAI
"to ransom for release by paying the ransom price" (Luke 24:21; 1 Peter 1:18)

LYTROSIS
"the act of freeing after the ransom is paid" (Luke 1:68; Hebrews 9:12)

APOLYTROSIS
"an act of setting free, deliverance, release" (Luke 21:28; Romans 3:24)

THE ROMANS ROAD TO SALVATION

The "Romans Road" explains God's plan of salvation using passages from the book of Romans.

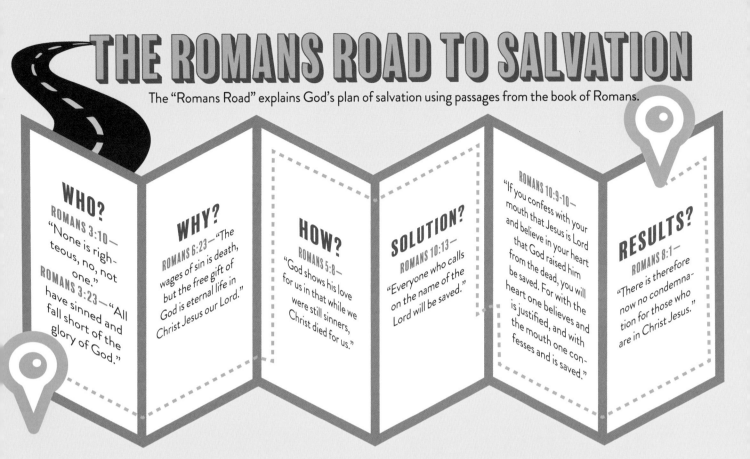

WHO?
ROMANS 3:10— "None is righteous, no, not one."
ROMANS 3:23— "All have sinned and fall short of the glory of God."

WHY?
ROMANS 6:23— "The wages of sin is death, but the free gift of God is eternal life in Christ Jesus our Lord."

HOW?
ROMANS 5:8— "God shows his love for us in that while we were still sinners, Christ died for us."

SOLUTION?
ROMANS 10:13— "Everyone who calls on the name of the Lord will be saved."

ROMANS 10:9-10— "If you confess with your mouth that Jesus is Lord and believe in your heart that God raised him from the dead, you will be saved. For with the heart one believes and is justified, and with the mouth one confesses and is saved."

RESULTS?
ROMANS 8:1— "There is therefore now no condemnation for those who are in Christ Jesus."

GOD, MAN, AND GOVERNMENT
(ROMANS 13:1-7)

- Everyone should subject themselves to governing authorities (13:1a)
- God is the ultimate authority (13:1b)
- Legitimate governments are the ones that *exist* (*de facto*) (13:1c)
- Government is instituted by God (13:1c)
- To resist government is to resist what God appointed (13:2)
- Resisting may bring about judgment (13:2b)
- Rulers are to promote good conduct and punish bad conduct (13:3)
- No need to be afraid of governing authorities if you do good (13:3b)
- Government officials are called to be servants of God (13:4)
- Those who do evil should be afraid because governing authorities may use weapons when needed (13:4)
- Governing authorities administer God's wrath on evildoers (13:4b)
- To obey the law is to do the right thing (13:5)
- Government officials are ministers of God (13:6)
- Citizens pay taxes to their government to help cover the costs of protection (13:6-7)

THE GREAT RESCUE

ADAM	JESUS
First Adam	Last Adam
Earthly man	Heavenly man
Garden of Eden	Garden of Gethsemane
Disobedience	Obedience
Brought sin	Brought salvation
Made man condemned	Made man savable
Sin enters the world	Grace available for all
Result is death	Result is life
Sin reigns	Grace reigns
Judgment for all	Gift for all
Condemnation	Justification

1 CORINTHIANS:
OUR SANCTIFICATION IN CHRIST

The epistle of 1 Corinthians is one of Paul's earliest works. It was written about 22 years after the crucifixion of Jesus and emphasizes the believer's sanctification. Paul had established the church at Corinth during his second missionary journey (Acts 18:1-17), but unfortunately, the people had reverted back to some of their worldly ways by the time Paul wrote this epistle. All scholars accept the Pauline authorship of this epistle as well as 2 Corinthians, Romans, and Galatians. Though the epistle is written as a corrective to the problems present in the Corinthian church, it provides valuable doctrinal information, including the early core message (known as the *kerygma*) of the church, spiritual gifts, and the nature of the resurrection body. The book can be divided in two sections: chapters 1–11 deal with the divisions, worldliness, and specific problems present in the congregation, and chapters 12–16 talk about spiritual order in the church, the gospel message, and the nature of the resurrection body.

QUICK FACTS

Date: AD 55–56
Theme: Sanctification in Christ (1:2)
Source: Paul wrote while in Ephesus (Acts 19:1, 10)
Recipients: The carnal (fleshly) church at Corinth in Achaia (Europe)

KEY WORDS: *Brethren, know, body, resurrection, church, Spirit, wisdom, wise, power*

KEY VERSE: "The natural person does not accept the things of the Spirit of God, for they are folly to him, and he is not able to understand them because they are spiritually discerned" (1 Corinthians 2:14).

KERYGMA

The *kerygma* (pronounced *cur-ig-ma*) is the early core message (or creed) of the gospel as stated in 1 Corinthians 15:1-7, and it predates Paul's writing of the epistle. Paul said he had "received" this message (verse 3), which was supported by more than 500 eyewitnesses. Thus, he could not have invented the *kerygma*. What is the *kerygma*? It is a creedal formula of statements that describe the core beliefs of the early church:

- "I delivered to you [the gospel] as of first importance what I also received:
- that Christ died for our sins in accordance with the Scriptures,
- that he was buried,
- that he was raised on the third day in accordance with the Scriptures,
- and that he appeared to Cephas,
- then [he appeared] to the twelve.
- Then he appeared to more than five hundred brothers at one time, most of whom are still alive, though some have fallen asleep.
- Then he appeared to James,
- then [he appeared] to all the apostles" (1 Corinthians 15:3-7).

GIFTS TO THE CHURCH

	1 Corinthians 12:8-11, 28	Romans 12:6-8	Ephesians 4:11-13; 1 Corinthians 12:28	1 Peter 4:9-11
Scripture	1 Corinthians 12:8-11, 28	Romans 12:6-8	Ephesians 4:11-13; 1 Corinthians 12:28	1 Peter 4:9-11
Greek Description	*Charismata*	*Charismata*	*Dorea*	*Charisma*
Source	The Holy Spirit	The Father	The Son	God
Purpose	Gifts given to people in the church	Gifts given to people in the church	People (offices) given as gifts to the church body	Gifts used in the church
Type of Gift	Spiritual exercise	Relational	Teaching and leadership	Practical service
Gifts	**Gifts**	**Gifts**	**Gifts**
	Word of wisdom	Prophecy	Apostle	Hospitality
	Word of knowledge	Serving	Prophet	Service
	Faith	Teaching	Evangelist	Teaching
	Healings	Exhortation	Pastor	
	Miracles	Giving	Teacher	
	Prophecy	Leadership		
	Discernment	Mercy		
	Tongues			
	Interpretation of tongues			
	Helps			
	Administration			

2 CORINTHIANS:
GOD IS OUR SUFFICIENCY

Paul wrote 2 Corinthians most likely less than a year after writing 1 Corinthians. In the letter he encourages the believers at Corinth to be triumphant in Christ (2:14). While the fact Paul was suffering at the time may have caused some to question his authority as an apostle, he uses it as an opportunity to justify his care and concern for God's people, a mark of a true apostle. After all, Christ suffered greatly in his ministry. The first epistle was a corrective aimed at addressing the many problems in the church, but the second emphasizes comfort, jubilation, and victory. Paul also touches upon several doctrines throughout the book, such as the substitutionary atonement of Christ (5:21), the afterlife (5:1-10), and giving to the church (8–9). In addition, he talks about false teachers in the church (11:13-15) and gives a robust justification of his apostleship (12:12). If the first epistle struck an objective and cerebral tone, the second was more subjective and heartfelt, revealing Paul's character and sentiment.

QUICK FACTS

Date: AD 55–56
Author: Paul
Location: Written in Philippi
Recipients: To the church at Corinth (Europe)
Theme: Be triumphant in Christ

KEY WORDS:
grace, comfort, afflict(ion), suffering, know, boast(ing), boldly, joy, rejoice

KEY VERSE:
"Thanks be to God, who in Christ always leads us in triumphal procession, and through us spreads the fragrance of the knowledge of him everywhere" (2 Corinthians 2:14).

OUTLINE

1. Comfort for ministers of Christ (1–2)
2. Comfort in the ministry (3–5)
3. Comfort to those who received the ministry (6–7)
4. Giving to the ministry (8)
5. Giving and its benefits for the ministry (9)
6. Justification of Paul's apostleship and ministry (10–13)

CHRIST, OUR OFFERING FOR SIN

Second Corinthians 5:21 communicates the incredible truth that Christ was presented as a sin offering on our behalf, taking on our sin so that we can take on his righteousness. This is what is meant by the substitutionary atonement. Unfortunately, some people have held to the confused notion that Christ remained sinless even until death. Here is what Scripture says:

Christ Was...

- Our substitute—he took the punishment that we deserved (Romans 6:23; Hebrews 10:10)
- Our sin offering—the Father placed our sin on Christ, who was sinless, and judged him as if Christ were us (John 3:16)
- Our judicial offering for sin—his sacrifice allowed God to pronounced us judicially innocent of sin (Romans 3:25-26)

Christ Was Not...

- Sinful—Jesus was sinless and without spot or blemish (Hebrews 4:15; 1 Peter 1:18-19)
- Evil—Jesus was holy, with no deceit found in his mouth (1 Peter 2:22)
- A sacrifice for his own sins—Jesus knew no sin (Hebrews 7:27)

🔑 KEY MESSAGES & THEMES:

- God's comfort of Paul in his affliction was used to comfort others (1:3-8)
- God delivers his people (1:10)
- God is sufficient (3:5)
- Christ is our atonement (5:12)
- We are to give generously to God's people (8–9)
- We are to take our thoughts captive to the obedience of Christ (10:4-5)
- The weakness Paul experienced in his sufferings made him stronger (12:10)

Principles of Giving

- Give yourself to the Lord first, then give to others (8:5)
- Develop a heart and passion for giving to others (8:3-4)
- Give according to your means, then test the Lord and go beyond (8:3)
- Be ready and willing to give (9:2)
- Give willingly, not from a sense of obligation (9:5)
- Give generously so that you may reap bountifully (9:6)
- Give cheerfully, not reluctantly (9:7)
- Giving brings abundance to the giver and blesses the recipient (9:8)
- Give with a thankful heart (9:10-11)

GALATIANS: FREEDOM IN CHRIST

The epistle to the Galatians was written to address incorrect teachings about salvation that had crept into one of the churches in Galatia. There is some debate as to which church it was, for Paul visited the region during all three of his missionary journeys. Of particular concern was that Judaizers (false teachers loyal to the law of Moses) were teaching the Galatians that circumcision was necessary for salvation (2:4; 5:2; 6:12). Because of this false doctrine, Paul conveyed fatherly concern that the believers in Galatia would return to their former legalistic belief systems. He explained the liberty that comes with salvation in Christ. They were no longer bound to the legalism that accompanied the Mosaic law (represented by Hagar) and were to go forward in freedom in Christ by faith alone (represented by Sarah) (4:21-31). A key phrase from Habakkuk 2:4—"the righteous shall live by his faith"—is emphasized in three books in the New Testament: Romans, Galatians, and Hebrews. Galatians emphasizes the practical aspect of the phrase, or the fact believers *shall live* by faith (3:11).

 **OUTLINE**

1. Freedom in Christ explained (1–2)
2. Freedom in Christ justified (3–4)
3. Freedom in Christ applied to life (5–6)

 **QUICK FACTS**

Date: AD 48
Author: Paul
Recipients: The church at Galatia
Theme: Liberty in Christ

KEY WORDS: *Believe, faith, Christ, circumcision, Christ, freedom, free, law, Spirit*

KEY VERSES: "Because of false brothers secretly brought in—who slipped in to spy out our freedom that we have in Christ Jesus, so that they might bring us into slavery—to them we did not yield in submission even for a moment, so that the truth of the gospel might be preserved in you" (Galatians 2:4-5).

FRUIT OF THE SPIRIT

Those who are led by the Spirit "will not gratify the desires of the flesh. For the desires of the flesh are against the Spirit, and the desires of the Spirit are against the flesh" (Galatians 5:16-17).

Fruit of the Spirit (Galatians 5:22-23)

 LOVE

 JOY

 PEACE

 PATIENCE

 KINDNESS

 GOODNESS

 FAITHFULNESS

 GENTLENESS

 SELF-CONTROL

Works of the Flesh (Galatians 5:18-21)

- Sexual immorality
- Impurity
- Sensuality
- Idolatry
- Sorcery
- Enmity
- Strife
- Jealousy
- Fits of anger
- Rivalries
- Dissensions
- Divisions
- Envy
- Drunkenness
- Sexual deviation
- Various things like those listed above

EPHESIANS: OUR POSITION IN CHRIST

One of the four epistles Paul wrote while in prison, Ephesians was addressed to the Christian church in Ephesus (1:1), where Paul labored for three years. This city was a commercial and cultic center in Asia Minor (Turkey). The residents were well known as zealous devotees to the cult of Diana (Roman name), or Artemis (Greek name). At one point, Paul's ministry efforts resulted in a riot by the followers of Diana, which led to his departure for Macedonia (Acts 19:24–20:1).

The epistle informs believers of their heavenly position in Christ (1:3), encourages unity in Christ (4:1-6), and urges love for one another in Christ, informing husbands and wives how they should act toward each other (5:22-33). Paul also exhorts all believers to stand fast in Christ, wearing the spiritual armor intended to protect them against the spiritual attacks of the devil (6:10-18).

Ephesians contains a simple outline that divides the book into two parts: Our position in Christ (1–3), and our walk in Christ (4–6). The first half of the book is doctrinal, and the second half emphasizes living out what is true about us.

QUICK FACTS

Author: Paul
Date: AD 60–62
Location: Written while in prison at Rome
Recipients: The church located in Ephesus (Turkey)
Theme: Our heavenly position (exaltation) in Christ

KEY WORDS:

Love, one, heavenly places, grace, Spirit, church, same body

KEY VERSE:

"Blessed be the God and Father of our Lord Jesus Christ, who has blessed us in Christ with every spiritual blessing in the heavenly places" (Ephesians 1:3).

THE ARMOR OF GOD IN EPHESIANS 6

Paul says the believer's spiritual armor is to be worn at all times. Our battle is not with mortal human beings, but against the forces of spiritual darkness (6:11-12). This kind of "warfare" requires a special set of equipment that only God provides.

Helmet of Salvation—Knowing you have been saved protects your mind from embracing false ideas to the contrary.

HELMET

Shield of Faith—Faith protects you from the continuous onslaught of poisonous temptations and ideas that can erode your confidence in Christ.

SHIELD

Breastplate of Righteousness—Your pure and righteous standing before God protects your heart against accusations that are untrue.

BREASTPLATE

Belt of Truth—Truth is the girdle that grounds you in reality and holds together all of what you believe about God. As such, it supports the rest of your armor, which depends on a factual understanding of your position and power in Christ.

BELT

Feet Prepared with the Gospel of Peace—Each believer should be prepared to share the gospel message, which brings peace between God and man and is the foundational message that should guide our path and direction in life.

SHOES

Sword of the Spirit—This is the Word of God, which is both an offensive (gospel) and defensive (apologetics) weapon that penetrates the heart deeply and slices away doubt to defeat the enemy.

SWORD

PHILIPPIANS: REJOICE IN CHRIST

Philippians was written to believers at the first church Paul and Silas established in Greece (Macedonia) during Paul's second missionary journey (Acts 16). Lydia, a businesswoman, and other prominent women formed the core of the fellowship (4:2; Acts 16:14-16). Philippi was a Roman colony named after Philip II of Macedon, Alexander the Great's father. The book is among the epistles Paul wrote during his first imprisonment in Rome (1:13, 19; 4:22). The letter encourages the church to rejoice in Christ (1:26; 4:4), offers an update on Paul's condition (1:19; 4:10), gives thanks to the Philippians for their gifts (2:25, 28; 4:15), and urges them to think and live as citizens of heaven (1:27; 3:20).

QUICK FACTS

Authors: Paul and Timothy
Date: AD 61–62
Location: Written in Rome while in prison
Recipients: The church in Philippi

CHRIST'S 2 NATURES

Jesus as God	Jesus as Man
Self-existing	Born of a woman
Divine attributes	Human attributes
Eternal	Temporal
Independent	Dependent
Unchanging nature	Changing nature
Infinite	Finite
Simple (no parts)	Composite (had parts)
Inexhaustible	Became tired and hungry
Unchanging emotions	Changing emotions
Cannot suffer	Can suffer
Immortal	Mortal
Spirit	Matter (physical body)
Omniscience	Limited knowledge
Omnipresent	Local presence
Omnipotent	Limited power
Could not be tempted	Faced temptation

KEY WORDS: *Christ, know(ledge), joy, rejoice, mind, think, attitude, abound*

KEY VERSE: "Rejoice in the Lord always; again I will say, rejoice" (Philippians 4:4).

OUTLINE

1. Salutation of greeting and prayer (1:1-11)
2. Paul's condition and reflections (1:12-30)
3. Pattern of humility for Christian living (2)
4. Motivation for Christian living (3)
5. Exhortations for Christian living (4)

THE INCARNATION OF CHRIST

Jesus, who is God, also took on the form of a man and exhibited both divine and human characteristics (Philippians 2:5-11). He is the God-man (Greek *theanthropos*); he is perfectly God and perfectly man. In the chart on the left, let's look at his deity and his humanity.

COLOSSIANS: THE SUFFICIENCY OF CHRIST

Like Ephesians, Philippians, and Philemon, the book of Colossians is one of the epistles Paul wrote while he was confined to house arrest in Rome. Whereas Ephesians emphasizes the church, and Philippians focuses on the emptying (Greek *kenoo*) of Christ in his incarnation, Colossians describes the fullness (Greek *pleroma*) of God in Christ.

Colossians presents Christ as sufficient and preeminent (2:15-17), making each believer complete with no need to add to what Christ has already accomplished on the believer's behalf. This "complete" status comes only through a personal relationship with Christ; thus, Paul emphasizes the prepositional phrase "in Christ" or "in him" or "in the Lord" all through the book. He also shares several "mysteries."

QUICK FACTS

Author: Paul
Date: AD 60–61
Location: Written in Rome while in prison, delivered by Tychicus and Onesimus (4:7-9)
Recipients: Gentile believers in Colossae (Turkey), who most likely shared the letter with the Laodiceans, who lived about 12 miles away (4:16)
Theme: Addresses false teaching and exhorts believers to recognize Christ as sufficient

KEY WORDS: *All, complete, faith(ful), wisdom, knowledge, mystery, on account of*

KEY VERSES: "In him the whole fullness of deity dwells bodily, and you have been filled in him, who is the head of all rule and authority" (Colossians 2:9-10).

PREPOSITIONS OF RELATIONSHIP— "IN CHRIST"

1:2 "brothers *in Christ*"
1:4 "your faith *in Christ*"
1:16 "*by him* all things were created"
1:17 "*in him* all things hold together"
1:19 "*in him* all the fullness of God was pleased to dwell"
1:22 "*in his body* of flesh"
2:5 "your faith *in Christ*"
2:6 "walk *in him*"
2:7 "rooted and built up *in him*"
2:9 "*in him* the whole fullness of deity dwells"
2:10 "you have been filled *in him*"
2:11 "*in him* also you were circumcised"
2:15 "triumphing over them *in him*"
3:18 "fitting *in the Lord*"
3:20 "pleases *the Lord*"
4:7 "fellow servant *in the Lord*"
4:17 "you have received *in the Lord*"

OUTLINE

1. Greetings and thanksgiving (1)
2. Avoid deception and recognize the preeminent Christ (2)
3. New life in Christ (3)
4. Practical instructions on living and final greetings (4)

PUT ON THE NEW SELF

Comparing the Old Self and New Self	
PUT OFF	PUT ON
Impurity	Kindness
Passion	Humility
Evil desire	Meekness
Covetousness	Patience
Anger	Forgiving one another
Wrath	Love each other
Slander	Thankfulness

1 THESSALONIANS:
THE EXPECTATION OF THE COMING OF CHRIST

Thessalonica was the capital of the Roman province of Macedonia (Europe), well-situated by a harbor and trade route that made it one of the most prosperous commercial centers in the region. Paul and Silas visited the city on their second missionary journey and reasoned with people in the synagogue for three weeks (Acts 17:1-3). Many Greeks and prominent women came to belief (Acts 17:4). But the church's growth was not without persecution (1 Thessalonians 1:6). As they turned from their pagan idols to Christ (1:9), the Jews and people in the area persecuted them for their faith, much like they did to Paul and Silas when they initially visited the city (Acts 17:5-14). Paul had to be quickly ushered away to Berea, where the Jewish mob from Thessalonica followed him (Acts 17:13). This made the Thessalonian church a shining example for all the other churches to follow (1 Thessalonians 1:8). The epistle is addressed to Gentile converts who were commended for their continued faith in Christ, and Paul exhorted them to live faithfully in light of Christ's coming.

QUICK FACTS

Author: Paul
Date: AD 50–51
Location: Written in Corinth
Recipients: To the church at Thessalonica
Theme: Live faithfully in light of Christ's coming

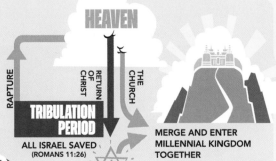

HEAVEN
RAPTURE
RETURN OF CHRIST
THE CHURCH
TRIBULATION PERIOD
ALL ISRAEL SAVED (ROMANS 11:26)
MERGE AND ENTER MILLENNIAL KINGDOM TOGETHER

OUTLINE

1. Greeting (1:1)
2. Commendation and encouragement (1–3)
3. Instruction, comfort, and exhortation (4–5)

A SIMPLIFIED
HISTORY OF ESCHATOLOGICAL VIEWS

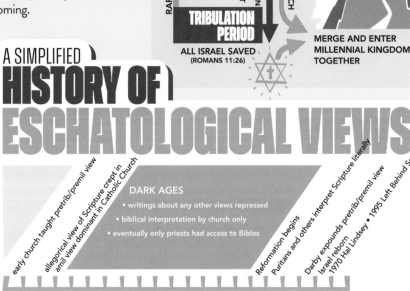

early church taught pretrib/premil view
allegorical view of Scripture crept in
amil view dominant in Catholic Church

DARK AGES
• writings about any other views repressed
• biblical interpretation by church only
• eventually only priests had access to Bibles

Reformation begins
Puritans and others interpret Scripture literally
Darby expounds pretrib/premil view
Israel reborn
1970 Hal Lindsey • 1995 Left Behind Series

0 AD 100 AD 200 AD 300 AD 400 AD 500 AD 600 AD 700 AD 800 AD 900 AD 1000 AD 1100 AD 1200 AD 1300 AD 1400 AD 1500 AD 1600 AD 1700 AD 1800 AD 1900 AD 2000 AD 2100

HIGHLIGHTS

1st century: early church taught pretrib/premil view
3rd century: allegorical view of Scripture crept in
4th century: amil view dominant in Catholic Church
4th century-1517: no other dominant views allowed/encouraged
1600-1700s: Puritans and others interpret Scripture literally
1800s: Darby and others revive and expound the pretrib/premil view
1900s: Scofield, Ironside, Walvoord advance the pretrib/premil view
Late 1900s: popular books educate lay people
   1970 *The Late Great Planet Earth* (Hal Lindsey)
   1995-2007 The Left Behind Series (Tim LaHaye)

KEY WORDS:
Love, gospel, spirit, faith, day of the Lord, coming, word, affliction

KEY VERSE:
"May the God of peace himself sanctify you completely, and may your whole spirit and soul and body be kept blameless at the coming of our Lord Jesus Christ" (1 Thessalonians 5:23).

2 THESSALONIANS:
THE DAY OF THE LORD

The second epistle to the Thessalonians continues one of the key themes of the first epistle, the second coming of Jesus Christ. Some of the believers in Thessalonica were afraid that the day of the Lord had already come (2:1-2), and Paul explained why this was not the case—this event was still future. He said that first there would be an apostasy, a falling away or rebellion, and that the Antichrist would rise on the scene before Christ's return (2:3). This person would be energized by Satan and have the ability to do false signs and wonders, and would persecute God's people (2:9). Paul added that the Holy Spirit's preserving influence on earth—as manifest through the lives of believers—is hindering this revelation. Only when the Spirit's influence is removed at the time of the rapture will the Antichrist be made known (2:6-8). Ultimately, the Antichrist, and the wicked with him, will be punished and destroyed in righteous judgment at Christ's return (1:5-9).

Paul also offered encouragement in light of the believers' ongoing persecution and affliction (1:4).

KEY WORDS:

Coming of Jesus Christ, faith, love, truth, glory, glorified, Spirit

KEY VERSES:

"We have confidence in the Lord about you, that you are doing and will do the things that we command. May the Lord direct your hearts to the love of God and to the steadfastness of Christ" (2 Thessalonians 3:4-5).

QUICK FACTS

Author: Paul
Date: AD 50–51
Location: Written in Corinth shortly after 1 Thessalonians
Recipients: The church at Thessalonica
Theme: The day of the Lord and the believers' glorification

OUTLINE

1. Greeting, thanksgiving, and comfort (1)
2. The day of the Lord (2)
3. Reassurance and commands to the congregation (3)

ORDER OF EVENTS

1 The great apostasy or rebellion occurs—many will fall away from the faith and follow sin (2:3)

2 The restrainer is removed at the time of the rapture and is no longer present to hold back the lawless one (2:6-7; cf. 2:1: "the coming of our Lord Jesus and our being gathered together to him")

3 The man of lawlessness is revealed—the Antichrist will be made known to the world (2:3-12)

4 The lawless one will be energized by Satan; he will be deceptive, performing false signs and wonders (2:9)

5 A strong delusion will be permitted by God—unbelievers who reject Christ will be deluded and deceived by the Antichrist, and will remain lost (2:10-12)

6 The Antichrist "will make a strong covenant with many for one week" (seven years) (Daniel 9:27)

7 The Antichrist will "put an end to sacrifice and offering" halfway into the covenant (Daniel 9:27)

8 The Antichrist will seat himself in the temple and proclaim himself to be God—this is the abomination of desolation (2:4; cf. Daniel 9:27; Matthew 24:15-16)

9 At this point the Great Tribulation will begin (Daniel 9:25-27; Matthew 24:15-51)

10 Jesus Christ will kill the Antichrist at his second coming and end the short but violent reign of the man of lawlessness (2:8; cf. Revelation 19:11-21)

1 TIMOTHY: ENCOURAGING FAITHFULNESS IN CHRIST

First Timothy is the first of three pastoral epistles, along with 2 Timothy and Titus. These were written after Paul's first imprisonment and during his second imprisonment in Rome. He wrote these epistles to encourage and direct his protégé, Timothy, a young, timid, and trusted convert from Lystra who had a grandmother named Lois, a Greek father (Acts 16:1), and Jewish mother named Eunice. Paul exhorted Timothy as a "child [or son] in the faith" (1:2) to stand up against false teachers who were imposing ascetic restrictions upon the believers at the church in Ephesus, where Timothy was a pastor (1:3-20). In addition, Paul also desired that Timothy be diligent in the ministry (1:18; 6:13-14) and teach believers how they ought to conduct themselves (2:8-15; 3:15).

QUICK FACTS

Author: Paul
Date: AD 64–66
Location: Written at an unknown location—most likely during Paul's undocumented fourth missionary journey
Recipients: Timothy and the church at Ephesus
Theme: Instructions on how to lead the church at Ephesus

OUTLINE

1. Greetings and confronting false teaching (1)
2. Encouragement to lead the church (2–3)
3. Identifying false teachers and instructions for the church (4–5)
4. Fight the good fight of faith (6)

KEY WORDS:

Faith, faithful, doctrine, godliness, good, sound, mercy, merciful

KEY VERSES: "Let no one despise you for your youth, but set the believers an example in speech, in conduct, in love, in faith, in purity. Until I come, devote yourself to the public reading of Scripture, to exhortation, to teaching" (1 Timothy 4:12-13).

QUALIFICATIONS FOR AN OVERSEER IN THE CHURCH

- ☑ 3:2—above reproach
- ☑ 3:2—the husband of one wife
- ☑ 3:2—sober-minded
- ☑ 3:2—self-controlled
- ☑ 3:2—respectable
- ☑ 3:2—hospitable
- ☑ 3:2—able to teach
- ☑ 3:3—not a drunkard
- ☑ 3:3—not violent but gentle
- ☑ 3:3—not quarrelsome
- ☑ 3:3—not a lover of money
- ☑ 3:4—manages his household well
- ☑ 3:4—with all dignity keeps his children submissive
- ☑ 3:5—cares for the church of God
- ☑ 3:6—not be a recent convert
- ☑ 3:6—not puffed up with conceit
- ☑ 3:7—must be well thought of by outsiders

QUALIFICATIONS FOR DEACONS IN THE CHURCH

- ☑ 3:8—dignified
- ☑ 3:8—not double-tongued
- ☑ 3:8—not addicted to much wine
- ☑ 3:8—not greedy for dishonest gain
- ☑ 3:9—must hold the mystery of the faith with a clear conscience
- ☑ 3:10—must be tested first
- ☑ 3:10—blameless
- ☑ 3:11—wives must be dignified
- ☑ 3:11—wives must be not slanderers
- ☑ 3:11—wives must be sober-minded
- ☑ 3:11—wives must be faithful in all things
- ☑ 3:12—the husband of one wife
- ☑ 3:12—manage their children and household well

2 TIMOTHY: PERSEVERANCE—
PAUL'S LAST WORDS TO TIMOTHY

Unlike Paul's first imprisonment in Rome, where he expected to be released and had several visiting friends, he had no expectation of being released from his second imprisonment under Emperor Nero (4:6-8). This epistle strikes a dire but personal tone; Paul has few friends left after being abandoned (1:15; 4:9-12), and these would be his last words to Timothy prior to his execution in AD 68. In this letter, Paul urges Timothy to hold fast and persevere in sound doctrine as he confronts false teachers (1:13-14). The Word of God should be the centerpiece of ministry in the church. Moreover, Paul expressed his desire to see Timothy again before his death, asking him to bring his jacket, books, and parchments (4:13-18).

QUICK FACTS

Author: Paul
Date: AD 66–67
Location: Written while imprisoned in Rome
Recipient: Timothy, his beloved son in the faith
Theme: Continue steadfast in the ministry of God's Word

OUTLINE

1. Greetings and encouragement in ministry (1)
2. Examples of endurance in ministry (2)
3. Persevere during difficult times in ministry (3)
4. Exhortations and encouragement to ministry (4)

KEY WORDS:
Faith, word, endure, gospel, diligent, sound, abide, unashamed

KEY VERSE:
"Follow the pattern of the sound words that you have heard from me, in the faith and love that are in Christ Jesus" (2 Timothy 1:13).

EXAMPLES OF ENDURANCE

Good Soldier—We are called to endure hardship like a soldier, who is singularly focused on achieving the mission at hand. Being sidetracked by other things can distract us from reaching the goal (2:1-2).

Athlete—We are to live the Christian life according to the biblical principles presented in God's Word, and not according to our own rules. Only then will we receive our reward (2:3-5).

Farmer—The steadfast, hard work accomplished by a farmer allows him to be the first to receive the reward of his crops. If we allow ourselves to become idle or lazy, we'll experience setbacks and receive no benefit from tasks that are left incomplete (2:6-13).

Worker—A diligent worker has nothing to be ashamed of at the end of the day. When we are diligent with God's Word, we will understand and handle it correctly (2:14-19).

Vessel—A vessel that is clean is useful. No one wants to eat from dirty dishes or use unsanitary vessels for presenting food to guests. This would bring shame and dishonor to the server. When we commit ourselves to walking in righteousness, we will receive honor from the Master (2:20-22).

Gentle Servant—Servants of Christ who are kind and gentle will not engage in argumentative behavior, but conduct themselves with humility, knowing that their positive demeanor can help with leading others to Christ (2:23-26).

TITUS: FAITH LEADS TO GOOD WORKS

Paul wrote this third and final pastoral epistle to his traveling companion, Titus, who is mentioned 13 times in Paul's epistles. An uncircumcised Greek from Antioch Syria, Titus received the gospel message from Paul (1:4; Galatians 2:3), then accompanied him on several trips, including to the Jerusalem council (Acts 15:2; Galatians 2:1-3) and on Paul's missionary journeys (2 Corinthians 7:6-7; 8:6, 16, 23). Titus was also sent by Paul to deal with problems in Corinth (2:12-13), and at the time this book is written, he was the pastor of the troubled church on the island of Crete (1:4-16).

This epistle emphasizes good works as proper behavior that flows from faith in Christ (2:2-10). Some doctrinal teachings are present, along with instructions about conduct in the church and how to address false teaching (1:9; 2:1-15; 3:2-14).

QUICK FACTS

Author: Paul
Date: Written between 1 and 2 Timothy in ca. AD 64
Location: Rome
Recipient: Titus, pastor of the church on Crete

Theme: Instructions and encouragement for Titus as he worked to set the church in order

KEY WORDS: *God, work(s), deed(s), sound doctrine, grace, Savior, faithful*

KEY VERSE: "Let our people learn to devote themselves to good works, so as to help cases of urgent need, and not be unfruitful" (Titus 3:14).

OUTLINE

1. Greeting, leadership, and false teachers (1)
2. Christian faith should lead to Christian conduct (2)
3. Final exhortations (3)

CONDUCT IN THE CHURCH

Older Men (2:2)

- Sober-minded
- Dignified
- Self-controlled
- Sound in the faith
- Sound in love
- Sound in steadfastness

Older Women (2:3-4)

- Reverent in behavior
- Not slanderers
- Not slaves to much wine
- Teachers of what is good
- Trainers of younger women

Younger Women (2:4-5)

- Love their husbands
- Love their children
- Self-controlled
- Pure
- Workers at home
- Kind
- Submissive to their husbands
- Conduct that prevents the Word of God from being reviled

Younger Men (2:6-8)

- Self-controlled
- A model of good works
- Teaches with integrity
- Shows dignity
- Speaks soundly in ways that cannot be condemned
- Nothing evil to say

Bondservants (2:9-10)

- Submissive to their masters in everything
- Well-pleasing
- Not argumentative
- Not pilfering
- Show good faith
- In everything, they adorn the doctrine of God our Savior

PHILEMON: THE TRANSFORMED LIFE IN CHRIST

This short letter was addressed to Philemon, his wife, Apphia, and his son, Archippus, who were wealthy slaveowners in Colossae (Colossians 4:9, 17). It was written at the same time as Colossians and Ephesians, during Paul's first Roman imprisonment (Acts 27–28). The letter was sent from Rome and delivered by Tychicus and Onesimus, who had become useful to Paul while he was in prison.

Onesimus had run away from Philemon's house, where a church met regularly (verse 2). Evidently he had stolen something of value (verse 18). After coming into contact with Paul, Onesimus became a believer and was transformed into a useful servant of Christ. Paul entreated Philemon to receive Onesimus back into his home not as a slave but as a "beloved brother" in Christ (verse 16). Paul used this epistle as an opportunity to touch upon key concepts related to salvation—being freed from slavery to sin and transformed by faith into a redeemed and useful servant of the Lord.

Paul went so far as to offer to pay any debt that had been owed to Philemon on Onesimus's behalf (verse 18). For Paul to send Onesimus back to Philemon was not an endorsement of slavery (slaves comprised over half the population of the Roman Empire), but a repudiation of the institution through the Judeo-Christian concepts of equality and fairness (Galatians 3:28; Ephesians 6:8), which would in time successfully undermine slavery as an institution.

KEY WORDS: *Grace, joy, love, accept, receive, have back, appeal*

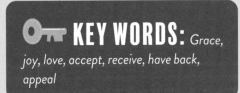

OUTLINE

1. Greetings (1-3)
2. Thanksgiving (4-7)
3. Petition to Philemon for Onesimus (8-22)
4. Salutation (23-25)

QUICK FACTS

Author: Paul
Date: AD 60–61
Location: Written while in prison in Rome
Recipients: Philemon, Apphia, and Archippus at Colossae
Theme: Redemption in Christ for useful service

KEY VERSES: "This perhaps is why he was parted from you for a while, that you might have him back forever, no longer as a bondservant but more than a bondservant, as a beloved brother—especially to me, but how much more to you, both in the flesh and in the Lord. So if you consider me your partner, receive him as you would receive me. If he has wronged you at all, or owes you anything, charge that to my account" (Philemon 15-18).

PAUL UNDERMINES SLAVERY

Some have criticized Paul for not being more outspoken about slavery. But the letter to Philemon implicitly conveys the Judeo-Christian principles that would eventually undermine and abolish this unethical and unbiblical institution worldwide.

- Paul did not approve of slavery, but implicitly undermined it (verse 16).
- He encouraged slaves to be obedient to their masters because this is a good testimony for the Lord (Titus 2:9-10).
- He encouraged slaves to act with humility toward their masters because this would reflect the character of Christ (Ephesians 6:5).
- He encouraged Christian masters to treat their slaves fairly because they would be held to account for mistreatment (Ephesians 6:9; see Exodus 21:20, 26; Ecclesiastes 12:14).
- He believed slaves and free persons were equal in Christ since we are all made in the image of God (Galatians 3:28; see Genesis 1:27).
- He declared that all people on the earth are "made from one man" (Acts 17:26) and we are "God's offspring" (Acts 17:29).
- He said all social classes are dissolved in Christ (Galatians 3:28).
- He said the slave Onesimus was his "very heart," which reflected Paul's innermost love for Onesimus (Philemon 12; see Romans 5:8).
- He encouraged Philemon to receive Onesimus "no longer as a bondservant" because this would be the morally right thing to do (Philemon 16).
- He encouraged Philemon to receive Onesimus as a "beloved brother" because they are equal in the eyes of God (Philemon 16; see Galatians 3:28).

HEBREWS: THE SUPERIORITY OF CHRIST OVER THE LAW

Hebrews is the first of eight general epistles, and unlike the Pauline epistles, which emphasize doctrine, they exhort believers and have a practical tone. Evidenced in this epistle is a sophisticated knowledge of Judaism and the Hebrew religious and cultural systems, which appears to indicate the book was written by a Jewish Christian to Jewish believers. It is possible the recipients were undergoing persecution (10:32-34) and in jeopardy of falling away from Christ and returning to the familiar ways of the old covenant (5:21–6:1; 7–10). Therefore, the author shows that Christ is greater than everything held sacred among religious Jews. Christ is portrayed as better than the prophets (1:1-3), angels (1:4–2:18), Moses (3), Joshua (4:1-13), priests (4:14–7:28), the tabernacle (8:1-5), the old covenant (8:6–9:22), and the animal sacrifices (9:23–10:39).

QUICK FACTS

Author: Unknown
Date: AD 60–69
Location: Unknown (Italy is suggested from Hebrews 13:24)
Recipients: Jewish Christians
Theme: Christ is greater than the law

KEY WORDS: God, eternal, forever, world, angels, better, covenant, faith, faithful, priest, priesthood, greater

KEY VERSE: "Let us leave the elementary doctrine of Christ and go on to maturity, not laying again a foundation of repentance from dead works and of faith toward God" (Hebrews 6:1).

OUTLINE

1. Jesus is greater than the angels (1–2)
2. Jesus is greater than the Mosaic law (3–10)
3. The life of faith and endurance (11–13)

JESUS IS A BETTER WAY

- Jesus is superior to the angels (1:2-14)—he is the Creator and the Son of God.
- Jesus has a superior message (2:1-4)—he is the message of the gospel, death, and resurrection.
- Jesus is superior to Moses (3:1-6)—he is the enduring Son of glory who cannot fade.
- Jesus is superior to Aaron (4:14–5:5)—he is our priest for eternity without change.
- Jesus is superior to Joshua (4:1-13)—he is the commander of the Lord of hosts.
- Jesus is superior to the priests (4:14–7:28)—he is our great high priest.
- Jesus is superior to the tabernacle (8:1-5)—he is not a ceremonial shadow of what saves; He is the substance and perfect fulfillment of the law.
- Jesus is superior to the old covenant (8:6–9:22)—he is written on the heart (ministry of reconciliation) and not only on stone (ministry of condemnation).
- Jesus is superior to the animal sacrifices (9:23–10:39)—he is the sinless lamb of God who brings salvation through his blood.
- Jesus is superior to the Levitical priesthood (7:9-28)—he is our divine, eternal, powerful, high priest who can save.

THE HALL OF FAITH (HEBREWS 11)

Hebrews 11:1-2: "Faith is the assurance of things hoped for, the conviction of things not seen. For by it the people of old received their commendation."

Person of Faith	Act of Faith	Result	Scripture	Old Testament Passage
Abel	Offered a more acceptable sacrifice	Righteousness	11:4	Genesis 4
Enoch	He pleased God	Will not die	11:5	Genesis 5
Noah	Built the ark	Heir of righteousness	11:7	Genesis 5
Abraham	Traveled to the land of promise	Inheritance of the land	11:8	Genesis 12–25
Sarah	Received the promise she would conceive when old	Innumerable descendants	11:11	Genesis 12–23
Abraham	Willing to sacrifice his son Isaac	Received Isaac back again	11:17	Genesis 22
Isaac	Bestowed blessings on Jacob and Esau		11:20	Genesis 17–35
Jacob	Blessed each of the sons of Joseph		11:21	Genesis 25–50
Joseph	Mentioned the exodus and gave instructions to carry his bones out of Egypt	The exodus occurred and his bones were carried with the Israelites	11:22	Genesis 37–50
Moses	Was hidden for three months	No fear of the king	11:23	Exodus 2
Moses	Refused to be called son of Pharaoh's daughter	Considered the reproach of Christ his wealth	11:24-26	Exodus 6–14
Moses	Left Egypt	Saw him who is invisible	11:27	
Moses	Kept the Passover and sprinkled the blood	Life for the firstborn	11:28	
Israelites	Crossed the Red Sea	Pharaoh and the Egyptian army were destroyed	11:29	
Israelites	Circled Jericho for seven days	The walls were destroyed	11:30	
Rahab	Received the spies peacefully	Survived Jericho's destruction	11:31	Joshua 2, 6
Gideon	Conquered kingdoms, enforced justice, obtained promises, stopped the mouths of lions, quenched the power of fire, escaped the edge of the sword, were made strong out of weakness, became mighty in war, and put foreign armies to flight. Women received back their dead by resurrection. Some were tortured, others suffered floggings, chains, and imprisonment. They were stoned, sawn in two, killed with the sword. They were destitute, afflicted, mistreated—of whom the world was not worthy.	Temporary deliverance of Israel from their oppressors	11:32-38	Judges 6–8
Barak				Judges 4–5
Samson				Judges 13–16
Jepthah				Judges 11–12
David				Ruth 4; 1 and 2 Samuel
Samuel				1 Samuel; 1 Chronicles 6; 9; 11; 26
The prophets				Old Testament prophetic books

JAMES: LIVING OUT YOUR FAITH

The epistle of James was written by the half brother of Jesus (1:1; Matthew 13:55) and is often considered to be the "Proverbs" of the New Testament due to its emphasis on wisdom and Christian living. Addressed to scattered Jewish Christians who were suffering persecution (1:2-3), James emphasizes prayer and wisdom for overcoming trials, which help produce patience and endurance in us (1:2-8). Further, we are to live out our faith, for our good works serve as evidence of our salvation. In addition, serving those in need is the essence of pure and undefiled religion (1:27).

James's emphasis on good works (2:14-26) has caused some to mistakenly believe the epistle contradicts Paul's emphasis on grace. Even Martin Luther placed James in the appendix of his 1522 translation of the New Testament. But it is clear that James addresses works that *follow from* salvation, while Paul emphasizes that there is no place for works in *receiving* salvation. Both authors are in agreement and address the issue of salvation from two distinct but complementary perspectives.

QUICK FACTS

Author: James
Date: AD 48–49
Location: Written in Jerusalem
Recipients: Jewish Christians who were dispersed in the surrounding areas and known as "the twelve tribes scattered among the nations" (1:1).
Themes: Pray for wisdom, living out your faith is evidence of salvation, pure religion is serving those in need

KEY WORDS:
Faith, brethren, deed, work, sin, perfect, wisdom, judge, judgment, law, sin

KEY VERSES:
"Count it all joy, my brothers, when you meet trials of various kinds, for you know that the testing of your faith produces steadfastness. And let steadfastness have its full effect, that you may be perfect and complete, lacking in nothing. If any of you lacks wisdom, let him ask God, who gives generously to all without reproach, and it will be given him" (James 1:2-5).

OUTLINE

1. Greetings and living the Christian life in the midst of trials (1)
2. Faith without works is dead (2–3)
3. Words and wisdom (3–4)
4. Judgment and patience (5)

THE 4 JAMES IN THE NEW TESTAMENT

1. James the son of Zebedee (Mark 1:19)—One of the 12 apostles and brother of the apostle John. He was martyred in Jerusalem in AD 44.

2. James the son of Alpheus (Mark 3:18)—One of the 12 apostles and possibly the brother of the apostle Matthew (Mark 2:14); also known as James "the younger" or "the Less."

3. James the father of Judas (Thaddaeus) (Luke 6:16)—He was one of the 12 apostles.

4. James, the half brother of Jesus (Matthew 13:55; Acts 15:13)—The writer of the epistle of James and the leader of the Jerusalem church. Died as a martyr in AD 62.

DISTINGUISHING FAITH AND WORKS IN PAUL AND JAMES

PAUL	JAMES
Romans 3:28: "We hold that one is justified by faith apart from works of the law." Romans 4:5: "To the one who does not work but believes in him who justifies the ungodly, his faith is counted as righteousness." Ephesians 2:8-9: "By grace you have been saved through faith. And this is not your own doing; *it is the gift of God, not a result of works, so that no one may boast.*"	James 2:20-24: "Do you want to be shown, you foolish person, that faith apart from works is useless? Was not Abraham our father justified by works when he offered up his son Isaac on the altar? You see that faith was active along with his works, and faith was completed by his works; and the Scripture was fulfilled that says, 'Abraham believed God, and it was counted to him as righteousness'—and he was called a friend of God. *You see that a person is justified by works and not by faith alone.*"
Spoke about faith and works from God's perspective	Spoke about faith and works from man's perspective
Faith necessarily precedes salvation	Works necessarily follow salvation
Works not needed for salvation because God sees the heart	Works need to follow salvation because man cannot see the heart
Paul speaks of justification in the eyes of God	James speaks of justification in the eyes of man
Salvation is through faith, which needs no works	Faith is completed (made perfect) by works
One is justified in the eyes of God	One is justified in the eyes of human onlookers
Abraham accounted righteous by faith apart from works while yet uncircumcised	Offers the example of Abraham offering his son Isaac; works accompanied Abraham's faith
Focus on faith necessary to *receive* salvation	Focus on works necessary to *follow* salvation
Paul addressed those who believed works of the law (or circumcision) were necessary for salvation and faith alone was not sufficient	James addressed those who believed that good deeds were not needed because faith was sufficient for salvation

WHAT IS SAVING FAITH? (JAMES 2:17)

DEAD FAITH	LIVING FAITH
Does not bring salvation	Brings salvation
Faith *that* Christ is the Messiah	Faith *in* Christ as Messiah
Faith is objective	Faith is subjective
Faith that perceives	Faith that receives
Matter of the mind	Matter of the mind and will
Mental understanding only	Mental understanding and heart belief
Faith that does not produce good works	Faith that produces good works
Acts of mere cogitation	Acts of volition, which follow cogitation

1 PETER: ENCOURAGEMENT
FOR THE SUFFERING CHURCH

First Peter is a letter of encouragement to the Jewish Christians of northern Asia Minor (Turkey, south of the Black Sea) who were suffering due to intense persecution. Peter presents arguments for Christian living while enduring hard times, with his appeal to the resurrected Christ as the foundation of living hope in all believers (1:3). The outcome of suffering is the hope of glory, which endures forever (2 Corinthians 4:17). To suffer unjustly with patience is precious in the sight of God; believers are called to suffer with endurance in this life (2:20; 3:13–4:11). Because Christ is set forth as our "example" (Greek *hupogrammos*) of suffering (2:21), we should follow in his steps. With this in mind, Peter commands his readers to reason with others about their faith and be ready to give an answer (Greek *apologia*) when someone asks about the living hope that is in them (1 Peter 3:15). He concludes his letter with a greeting and an encouragement that God is aware of their suffering, and in due time, he will strengthen and heal them (5:10).

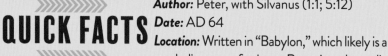

QUICK FACTS

Author: Peter, with Silvanus (1:1; 5:12)
Date: AD 64
Location: Written in "Babylon," which likely is a symbolic term referring to Rome in order to disguise Peter's location from persecutors (5:13)
Recipients: Pilgrims of the dispersion (Jewish Christians) in Asia Minor (Turkey), which included Pontus, Galatia, Cappadocia, Asia, and Bithynia (1:1)
Themes: Persevere and understand suffering in the midst of persecution

🔑 KEY WORDS:
Grace, glory, glorify, submissive, suffer, suffering, trial, Spirit, time, live, life, love

🔑 KEY VERSE:
"After you have suffered a little while, the God of all grace, who has called you to his eternal glory in Christ, will himself restore, confirm, strengthen, and establish you" (1 Peter 5:10).

OUTLINE

1. Understand suffering (1)
2. Christ is our example in suffering (2)
3. Submission in suffering (2–3)
4. Exhortation to persevere in suffering (3–4)
5. Greetings and encouragement in suffering (5)

15 THINGS
TO REMEMBER ABOUT CHRIST'S EXAMPLE AND SUFFERING

1. We are called to suffer patiently
2. We should follow in Christ's footsteps
3. Christ did not sin in word or deed
4. When reviled, Christ did not revile in return
5. When made to suffer, Christ did not threaten
6. Christ trusted God, who is the righteous judge
7. Christ accomplished spiritual healing and forgiveness through suffering
8. We are to exhibit humility under the mighty hand of God
9. We will be exalted in due time
10. We are to cast our cares upon God
11. God cares for us
12. We are to be sober-minded
13. We are to resist the devil
14. We are to remain firm in our faith
15. We are to remember that other believers are suffering as well

2 PETER: GODLY LIVING AND PERSEVERING IN THE TRUTH

Prior to his execution in Rome, Peter writes his farewell testimony to those who have attained faith in Christ (1:1). These are most likely the same "exiles of the Dispersion" in northern Asia Minor as mentioned in 1 Peter 1:1. Here, Peter makes clear that God's grace and the Holy Spirit are the foundations for godly living and action. Peter addresses several topics, including warnings against impurity and reminders of Christian virtue (1:1-15), Christ's authority (1:16-21), apostasy and false teachers (2), and the importance of godly Christian living in light of Christ's return (3). Peter also mentions the day of the Lord as a coming time when Christ will judge the ungodly (3:7). In all this, Peter sobers his readers and urges them to live godly and persevere in the truth because Christ will bring rewards and punishments (2:6-7). A significant emphasis of this epistle, then, is the sanctification of the believer.

QUICK FACTS

Author: Peter
Date: AD 64–67
Location: Rome
Recipients: To those of like precious faith, most likely in Pontus, Galatia, Cappadocia, Asia, and Bithynia (1:1; 3:1)
Themes: Living godly and preserving the truth in light of the Lord's coming

PETER

KEY WORDS:

Interpretation (Greek *epilyseos*)—means "unloosing" or "origin." Scripture was not initiated by man.

Produced (Greek *genetai*) means "come into being." Scripture did not come from man, who was the instrumental cause, but from God, who was the efficient primary cause.

Carried along (Greek *pheromenoi*) means "being borne along" or "being moved along." The Holy Spirit came upon (much like the way that wind pushes along the sails of a ship; cf. Acts 27:15, 17) yielded human writers who allowed the Spirit to direct and work through them.

KEY VERSES:

"Be all the more diligent to confirm your calling and election, for if you practice these qualities you will never fall. For in this way there will be richly provided for you an entrance into the eternal kingdom of our Lord and Savior Jesus Christ" (2 Peter 1:10-11).

DESCRIPTIONS OF THE DAY OF THE LORD

- Scoffers will ask, "Where is the promise of his coming?"
- The ungodly will be judged and destroyed.
- The Lord is not slow concerning his return, but is patient, not wanting any to perish.
- The day of the Lord will come like a thief (unexpectedly).
- The heavens will pass away with a roar.
- A new heaven and a new earth will emerge.

OUTLINE

1. Godly living by the grace of God (1)
2. False prophets and teachers (2)
3. Christ's return in the day of the Lord (3)

THE PROCESS OF INSPIRATION OF SCRIPTURE

"No prophecy of Scripture comes from someone's own interpretation. For no prophecy was ever produced by the will of man, but men spoke from God as they were carried along by the Holy Spirit" (2 Peter 1:20-21).

1, 2, AND 3 JOHN: WALKING IN THE LIGHT, LOVE, AND TRUTH

Some have suggested, without verification, that all three of the Johannine epistles were preserved as one unit to be read in the churches. But most agree that 1 John was to be read in all the churches, and 2 and 3 John, which are more personal in tone, were written to deal with specific needs in the local churches to which they were addressed.

The three epistles focus on believers' relationships with God and each other. The dominant themes are light, love, and truth. First John urges readers to walk in the light (1 John 1–2), dwell in divine love (3–4), and summons believers to understand and dwell in faith (5). Second John introduces the author as the "elder" (verse 1), as he had aged significantly by this time, and its recipients as the "elect lady and her children," referring to the house-church in Asia Minor (Turkey). In the second epistle, John expresses his delight that the church is walking in the truth (verse 4) and encourages his readers to continue walking in the truth and in love (verses 5-6). This love must be anchored to the truth of Christ's commandments (verse 6). Here, John strikes a balance between love and truth—namely, truth without love can be dogmatic and cold, and love without truth can become untethered to reality, even allowing false teachers to settle in the church in the name of love (verses 7-11).

QUICK FACTS

Author: John
Date: AD 85–95
Location: Ephesus
Recipients: Churches in Asia Minor
Theme: Encouragement to walk in light, life, love, and truth

KEY WORDS: Love, truth, true, darkness, light, life, walk, beloved, abide, God, sin, born of God

KEY VERSES: "If we walk in the light, as he is in the light, we have fellowship with one another, and the blood of Jesus his Son cleanses us from all sin" (1 John 1:7).

"This is love, that we walk according to his commandments; this is the commandment, just as you have heard from the beginning, so that you should walk in it" (2 John 6).

"Beloved, it is a faithful thing you do in all your efforts for these brothers, strangers as they are, who testified to your love before the church. You will do well to send them on their journey in a manner worthy of God. For they have gone out for the sake of the name, accepting nothing from the Gentiles. Therefore we ought to support people like these, that we may be fellow workers for the truth" (3 John 5-8).

First and 2 John offer a test for orthodoxy, appealing to Christ's resurrection body as the central truth to which love and truth must correspond (1 John 4:2; 2 John 7). Anything opposed to this is deception in the spirit of Antichrist (1 John 4:3; 2 John 7).

In 3 John, the author again refers to himself as the "elder" (verse 1). This is a personal letter dealing with a problem in the church between two individuals: Gaius, a faithful servant walking in love and truth (verse 1), and Diotrephes, a selfish person who is working against fellow believers in the church (verses 1, 9-10). The letter, delivered by Demetrius (verse 12), contains John's message to Gaius to continue steadfastly in response to opposition by walking in the truth (verses 3-4).

OUTLINE OF 1 JOHN

Purpose: To encourage believers to walk and dwell in light and love

1. Walk in the light (1–2)
2. Dwell in love (3–4)
3. Call to understanding and walk in faith (5)

OUTLINE OF 2 JOHN

Purpose: To exhort believers to walk in love according to the truth; to warn of false teachers who reject the fact of Christ's physical resurrection

1. Greeting (1-3)
2. Walking in truth and love (4-11)
3. Final greetings (12-13)

OUTLINE OF 3 JOHN

Purpose: To commend Gaius and expose Diotrephes's prideful behavior

1. Greetings and joy (1-4)
2. Praise for Gaius (5-8)
3. Diotrephes's opposition (9-10)
4. Demetrius's good testimony (11-12)
5. Final greetings and desire to meet (13-15)

JOHN

LIFE, LIGHT, LOVE, AND TRUTH

- **LIFE** (Greek *zoe*) is mentioned 135 times in the New Testament. It is used in reference to the very life of Christ himself (1 John 1:2), which he imparts to us when we place our faith in him. This life energizes, transforms, and animates us not only in a biological sense (*bios*), its ethical and spiritual vitality culminate in eternal life.

- **LIGHT** (*phos*) is often used in John's epistles and Gospel to refer to spiritual, intellectual, and moral illumination as well as to God's nature (1 John 1:5; John 8:12).

- **LOVE** (*agape*) is used throughout John's epistles to describe the unconditional love directed toward someone who doesn't inherently possess an attribute that is lovable. This love is duty-centered and involves the will and a heart of sacrifice (2 John 7; see also Romans 5:8). John says love is the essence of God's nature (1 John 4:7-8).

- **TRUTH** (*aletheia*) is used throughout the New Testament and prolifically in John's epistles (2 John 1; 3 John 1-3). In the original Greek text, this is a compound word that, in its negative form, means "not hidden" or "not concealed." In its positive usage, it refers to "that which corresponds to reality as it exists." To speak truth is to ground or anchor one's expressions or statements in the real world—to tell it like it is.

JUDE: CONTENDING FOR THE FAITH

Jude was the brother of James, and both were half brothers of Jesus (Matthew 13:55; Acts 1:14). This short epistle offers a powerful warning against apostasy (falling away) and false teachers.

This bold but reassuring letter presents readers with the assurance that God will preserve the faithful and that victory over all apostasy will occur at Christ's second coming. In the meantime, Jude encourages the church to persevere in the truth and prayer, and to battle against false teachers and avoid their teachings. Because Jude (verses 6-7) appears to rely on 2 Peter 2:5-7, which was penned around the mid-60s AD, and because there is no mention of the destruction of the Jerusalem temple by the Romans in AD 70, it is clear the epistle must have been written prior to AD 70 and after Peter's second epistle.

QUICK FACTS

Author: Jude
Date: AD 67–69
Location: Unknown
Recipients: Jewish and Gentile Christians in the region of Antioch

Themes: Confront apostasy and defend the faith against false teachers in the church

KEY WORDS: *Ungodly, ungodliness, judgment, eternal, everlasting, faith, beloved*

KEY VERSE: "Beloved, although I was very eager to write to you about our common salvation, I found it necessary to write appealing to you to contend for the faith that was once for all delivered to the saints" (Jude 3).

OUTLINE

1. Greeting (1-2)
2. Contending for the faith (3-4)
3. Examples of apostasy (5-7)
4. Descriptions of false teachers (8-16)
5. Consequences of apostasy (17-23)
6. Ultimate victory over apostasy (24-25)

Jude's DESCRIPTIONS OF FALSE TEACHERS (VERSES 8-16)

- Creep into the church unnoticed
- Designated for condemnation
- Ungodly
- Pervert the grace of God into sensuality
- Deny the Lord and master Jesus Christ

- Rely on dreams
- Defile the flesh
- Reject authority
- They blaspheme
- Will be destroyed
- Hidden reefs at love feasts
- Feast without fear or reverence
- Shepherds feeding themselves
- Waterless clouds
- Swept along by whichever way the winds blow

- Fruitless trees in late autumn
- Twice dead and uprooted
- Wild waves of the sea casting up the foam of their own shame
- Wandering stars
- Reserved for outer darkness
- Grumblers
- Malcontents
- Follow their sinful desires
- Loud-mouthed boasters
- Show favoritism to gain advantage

REVELATION: JUDGMENT AND CHRIST REVEALED

The book of Revelation unveils the Lord Jesus Christ and the consummation of all things. John was instructed to divide the book into three sections: (1) the things that he *has* seen, (2) the things that *are*, and (3) the things that are to take place *after this* (1:19). Thus the contents of this book speak of the past (1), the present (2–3), and the future (4–22).

CHAPTER 1 presents a past (previously established in the person and ministry of Christ) portrait of the person of Christ as the preeminent king, Alpha and Omega, firstborn of the dead, and the one who will save the righteous and judge the wicked.

CHAPTERS 2–3 proclaim warnings and rewards to the seven churches of Asia Minor located at Ephesus, Smyrna, Pergamos, Thyatira, Sardis, Philadelphia, and Laodicea.

CHAPTERS 4–22 present a vision of future events that describe an unprecedented time of divine judgments that will increase in intensity until their culmination in the second coming of Christ to the earth (19).

CHAPTERS 20–22 describe the 1,000-year reign of Christ; the judgment of the wicked; the incarceration of the devil, beast, and the false prophet; and finally, the arrival of the new heaven and new earth, along with the new Jerusalem (21), with its river of life and tree of life (22).

Revelation concludes with a sober declaration that the time is at hand and blessed are those who keep the words of prophecy written in the book (22:7). That is followed by warnings to not alter a word of this prophecy lest the plagues described within come upon those who do this (22:18-19).

QUICK FACTS

Author: John
Date: AD 90–96
Location: Isle of Patmos
Recipients: The seven churches in Asia Minor located at Ephesus, Smyrna, Pergamos, Thyatira, Sardis, Philadelphia, and Laodicea
Theme: Divine judgment on the wicked and the unveiling of the Lord Jesus Christ

KEY WORDS:
Nations, thunder, after, these things, dragon, God, Jesus, lamb, angel, devil, Satan, beast, church, plague, Spirit, sound, voice, wrath, seal, repent, woe

KEY VERSE:
"Write therefore the things that you have seen, those that are and those that are to take place after this" (Revelation 1:19).

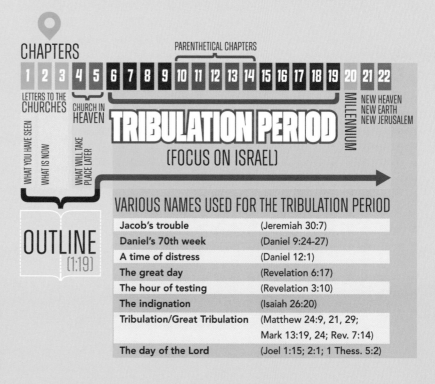

CHAPTERS

1 2 3 | 4 5 | 6 7 8 9 10 11 12 13 14 15 16 17 18 19 | 20 | 21 22

LETTERS TO THE CHURCHES | CHURCH IN HEAVEN | PARENTHETICAL CHAPTERS (10–14) | MILLENNIUM | NEW HEAVEN NEW EARTH NEW JERUSALEM

WHAT YOU HAVE SEEN | WHAT IS NOW | WHAT WILL TAKE PLACE LATER

TRIBULATION PERIOD
(FOCUS ON ISRAEL)

OUTLINE (1:19)

VARIOUS NAMES USED FOR THE TRIBULATION PERIOD

Jacob's trouble	(Jeremiah 30:7)
Daniel's 70th week	(Daniel 9:24-27)
A time of distress	(Daniel 12:1)
The great day	(Revelation 6:17)
The hour of testing	(Revelation 3:10)
The indignation	(Isaiah 26:20)
Tribulation/Great Tribulation	(Matthew 24:9, 21, 29; Mark 13:19, 24; Rev. 7:14)
The day of the Lord	(Joel 1:15; 2:1; 1 Thess. 5:2)

THE SEVEN CHURCHES OF ASIA MINOR

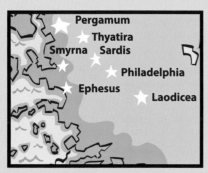

Pergamum
Thyatira
Smyrna Sardis
Philadelphia
Ephesus
Laodicea

THE JUDGMENTS OF
REVELATION

● SEAL JUDGMENTS ● TRUMPET JUDGMENTS ● BOWL JUDGMENTS

	RAPTURE		MIDPOINT	
		3.5 YEARS		3.5 YEARS
CHURCH AGE	VIEW 1	SEALS	TRUMPETS	BOWLS
	VIEW 2	SEALS		TRUMPETS	BOWLS
	VIEW 3	SEALS	TRUMPETS	BOWLS

GAP PERIOD DURATION UNKNOWN

7-YEAR TRIBULATION PERIOD BEGINS WITH TREATY AND ENDS WITH RETURN OF CHRIST

INTERESTING FACTS
ABOUT THE NEW JERUSALEM

HEIGHT, WIDTH, DEPTH
1,380 miles each direction

CUBE VS. PYRAMID
Pyramids associated with occult and sun worship
Cube associated with God's presence/temple/Holy of Holies

FUNCTIONAL CONSTRUCTION
Resurrected bodies not subject to gravity
"Streets" may include vertical passageways
City "blocks" may be cubes as well
The city will match how bodies function

CAPACITY
The New Jerusalem could house 20 billion people
averaging 75 acres per person (using only 25% of the city)

Calculations taken from *The Revelation Record* by Dr. Henry Morris
(Carol Stream, IL: Tyndale House Publishers, 1983), 450-451

CAMPAIGN OF
ARMAGEDDON

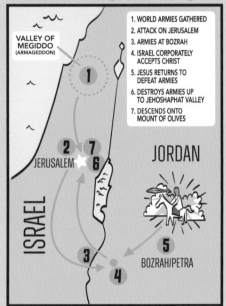

VALLEY OF MEGIDDO (ARMAGEDDON)

1. WORLD ARMIES GATHERED
2. ATTACK ON JERUSALEM
3. ARMIES AT BOZRAH
4. ISRAEL CORPORATELY ACCEPTS CHRIST
5. JESUS RETURNS TO DEFEAT ARMIES
6. DESTROYS ARMIES UP TO JEHOSHAPHAT VALLEY
7. DESCENDS ONTO MOUNT OF OLIVES

JERUSALEM

ISRAEL

JORDAN

BOZRAH/PETRA

FINAL
KEY EVENTS

- Battle of Armageddon/defeat of the nations
- Beast and false prophet thrown into lake of fire
- Earth renovated/God's people ruling with him

- Satan released for last battle
- Satan thrown into lake of fire
- Great White Throne judgment
- New heavens/new earth
- New Jerusalem

CHURCH AGE

MILLENNIAL KINGDOM

ETERNAL STATE

TRIBULATION

PART 3

BIBLE HISTORY, THE MESSIAH, AND THE FUTURE

OLD TESTAMENT FIGURES CONFIRMED BY
ARCHAEOLOGY

PERSON	SCRIPTURES	TIME PERIOD	SOURCES
King Ahab	I Kings 16:28-33; 21:1, 22; 22:28	9th century BC	Mesha Stele Kurkh Monolith Palace in Samaria
King Ahasuerus (Xerxes I)	Esther 1:1-2	5th century BC	Silver bowl inscription of Artaxerxes I Palace wall relief at Persepolis (Iran) Elephantine Papyri Tomb at Persepolis
King Ahaz/ Achaz	2 Kings 16:2; Matthew 1:9	8th century BC	Stamp seal (bulla)
Ahikam	2 Kings 22:12	7th century BC	Stamp seal (bulla)
Amariah	2 Chronicles 31:15	8th–7th century BC	Stamp seal (bulla)
King Artaxerxes I (Longimanus)	Ezra 4:7; 7:1-21; Nehemiah 2:1; 5:14; 13:6	5th century BC	Silver bowl inscription of Artaxerxes I Elephantine Papyri Tomb at Persepolis
Asaiah	2 Kings 22:12, 14; 2 Chronicles 34:20		Stamp seal (bulla)
King Ashurbanipal (Osnapper)	Ezra 4:10; 2 Chronicles 33:10-13	7th century BC	1,200 texts from the library of Nineveh Stela of Ashurbanipal Nineveh palace reliefs
Azaliah	2 Kings 22:3	7th century BC	Stamp seal (bulla)
Azzur	Jeremiah 28:1	7th–6th century BC	Stamp seal (bulla)
King Ba'alis	Jeremiah 40:14	6th century BC	Stamp seal (bulla)
Balaam	Numbers 22–24; Jude 11; Revelation 2:14	15th–14th century BC	Balaam Inscription (1967)
Baruch (Jeremiah's Scribe)	Jeremiah 32:12-16	7th century BC	Stamp seal (bulla)
King Belshazzar (Son of Nabonidus)	Daniel 5; 7:1; 8:1	6th century BC	Nabonidus Chronicle Cylinder of Nabonidus
Ben Hadad II	2 Kings 8:7-13; 13:1-3	9th century BC	Tel Dan Stele Black Obelisk of Shalmaneser III
King Cyrus II	2 Chronicles 36:22–23; Ezra 1:1-8; Isaiah 44:28; 45:1	6th century BC	Tomb at Pasargadae Cyrus Cylinder Cyrus brick inscriptions
King Darius I (Son of Hystaspes)	Ezra 4:5, 24	6th–5th century BC	Tomb at Persepolis Behistun Inscription Elephantine Papyri
King Darius (the Persian)	Nehemiah 12:22	5th century BC	Silver bowl inscription of Artaxerxes I Behistun Inscription Palace wall relief at Persepolis (Iran)
King David	1 Samuel 16:13; 2 Samuel 5:3-7	10th century BC	Tel Dan Stele Mesha Stele
Eliakim	2 Kings 18:18-37; 19:2	6th century BC	Stamp seal (bulla)
Elishama	Jeremiah 36:12-21	6th century BC	Stamp seal (bulla)
Elnathan	Ezra 8:16	5th century BC	Stamp seal (bulla)
King Esarhaddon	2 Kings 19:37; Ezra 4:2; Isaiah 37:38	7th century BC	Royal brick inscription Esarhaddon Chronicle Stone prism of Esarhaddon Stone lion's head with inscription Wall relief of Esarhaddon and queen mother Letters of Esarhaddon
King Evil-Merodach (Amel Marduk)	2 Kings 25:27; Jeremiah 52:31	6th century BC	Jehoiachin ration record
Gedaliah (Son of Ahikam)	2 Kings 25:22-25; Jeremiah 39:14; 40:5-16; 41; 43:6	6th century BC	Stamp seal (bulla)
Gedaliah (Son of Pashhur)	Jeremiah 38:1	7th–6th BC	Stamp seal (bulla)
Gemariah	Jeremiah 29:3; 36:10-12, 25	6th century BC	Stamp seal (bulla) Lachish Letters?
Name Similar to Goliath	1 Samuel 17	11th–9th century BC	Gath inscription
Hananiah	Jeremiah 28:1	7th–6th century BC	Stamp seal (bulla)
Priestly Family Name of Immer	Jeremiah 20:1; 38:1	7th–6th century BC	Stamp seal (bulla)
King Hazael	2 Kings 8:7-15; 12:17	9th century BC	Tel Dan Stele Black Obelisk of Shalmaneser III Gath siege trench ivory decoration Inscription at Khadatu
King Hezekiah	2 Kings 16:20; 18:1-2	8th–7th century BC	Stamp seal (bulla) Annals of Sennacherib Taylor Prism The Azekah Inscription Jerusalem broad wall water tunnel system
Hilkiah (High Priest)	2 Kings 22:4-14; 23:4, 24	7th century BC	Stamp seal (bulla)
Pharaoh Hophra (Apries)	Jeremiah 44:30	6th century BC	Herodotus's Histories Tablet reliefs from Abydos Palace at Memphis Babylonian Chronicle
King Hoshea	2 Kings 15:30; 17:1	8th century BC	Stamp seal (bulla) Assyrian records of Tiglath-pileser III
Son of Immer	Jeremiah 20:1	7th–6th century BC	Two stamp seals (bullae)
Jaazaniah	2 Kings 25:23; Jeremiah 40:8	7th–6th century BC	Stamp seal (bulla)

PERSON	SCRIPTURES	TIME PERIOD	SOURCES
King Jehoahaz (or Shallum)	2 Kings 23:30-34; 1 Chronicles 3:15; 2 Chronicles 36:1 ff.	7th century BC	Stamp seal (bulla)
King Jehoiachin (Coniah)	2 Kings 24:8-15; 2 Chronicles 36:8 ff.; Jeremiah 22:24, 28; 37:1	6th century BC	Jehoiachin ration record Babylonian Chronicles Jar handles stamped with his name at Tell Beit Mirsim and at Beth-Shemesh
King Jehu (or Joram)	1 Kings 19:16-17; 2 Kings 9:20; 10:31	9th century BC	Black Obelisk of Shalmaneser III
Jerahmeel	Jeremiah 36:26	7th century BC	Stamp seal (bulla)
Jehucal	Jeremiah 37:3; 38:1	6th century BC	Stamp seal (bulla)
King Jeroboam II (son of Jehoash)	2 Kings 13:13; 1 Chronicles 5:17; Amos 1:1; 7:9-11	8th century BC	Stamp seal (bulla)
Queen Jezebel	1 Kings 16:31; 21; 2 Kings 9	9th century BC	Stamp seal (bulla) Palace in Samaria
Joezar and Igdaliah	Jeremiah 35:4; cf. 1 Chronicles 12:7	7th century BC	Stamp seal (bulla)
King Jotham (Son of Uzziah)	2 Kings 15:32	8th century BC	Stamp seal (bulla)
Malchiah	Jeremiah 38:6	7th–6th century BC	Stamp seal (bulla)
King Manasseh (Son of Hezekiah)	2 Kings 20:21; 21; 2 Chronicles 33:10-11	7th century BC	Stamp seal (bulla) Prism B of Esarhaddon
King Menahem	2 Kings 15:14-23	8th century BC	Assyrian records of Tiglath-pileser III
King Merodach-Baladan (Babylon)	2 Kings 20:12; Isaiah 39:1	8th century BC	Marble boundary stone Annals of Sargon of Assyria Sennacherib Prism
King Mesha (Moab)	2 Kings 3:4	9th century BC	Mesha Stele aka Moabite Stone
Meshullum	2 Kings 22:3	7th century BC	Stamp seal (bulla)
Nathan-melech	2 Kings 23:11	7th century BC	Stamp seal (bulla)
King Nebuchadnezzar (Babylon)	2 Kings 24:1-11; Daniel 1:1; 2; 3; 4:34-37; 5	7th–6th century BC	Royal brick inscriptions Ishtar Gate Babylonian Chronicles Behistun Inscription East India House Inscription
Pharaoh Necho	2 Chronicles 35:20-22; 36:4	7th–6th century BC	Statues of Necho Herodotus's *Histories* Necho's name removed from monuments by son Psammetichus II
Neriah	Jeremiah 36:32	7th–6th century BC	Stamp seal (bulla)
King Omri	1 Kings 16:16-30; 2 Kings 8:26; 2 Chronicles 22:2; Micah 6:16	9th century BC	Black Obelisk of Shalmaneser III Mesha Stele
Pedaiah	1 Chronicles 3:18 ff.	6th century BC	Stamp seal (bulla)
King Pekah	2 Kings 15:27	8th century BC	Assyrian records of Tiglath-pileser III

PERSON	SCRIPTURES	TIME PERIOD	SOURCES
Tiglath-Pileser III (Pul)	2 Kings 15:19, 29; 1 Chronicles 5:6; 2 Chronicles 28:20	8th century BC	Palace wall relief Assyrian records of Tiglath-pileser III
Sanballat	Nehemiah 2:10	5th century BC	Elephantine Papyri Stamp seal (bulla)
King Sargon II	Isaiah 20:1	8th century BC	Winged Bull of Sargon II Palace of Sargon (Khorsabad) Annals of Sargon Royal Brick Inscription
Sarsekim	Jeremiah 39:3	6th century BC	Cuneiform tablet at British Museum
King Sennacherib (Assyria)	2 Kings 18:13; 19:16-36; 2 Chronicles 32; Isaiah 36:1; 37	8th–7th century BC	Royal Brick Inscription Annals of Sennacherib Taylor Prism Sargon's Palace reliefs
Seriah	Jeremiah 51:59	7th–6th century BC	Stamp seal (bulla)
Shaphan	2 Kings 22:12	7th century BC	Stamp seal (bulla)
Shebna	2 Kings 18:18-37; Isaiah 22:15-25	8th century BC	Royal Steward (tomb lintel) Inscription
Shelemiah	Jeremiah 37:3	7th–6th century BC	Stamp seal (bulla)
Shelomith	1 Chronicles 3:19	5th century BC	Stamp seal (bulla)
Pharaoh Shishak (Shossheq I)	1 Kings 11:40; 14:25; 2 Chronicles 12:2-9	10th century BC	Karnak Temple of Amun reliefs
Pharaoh Tirhakah (Taharqa)	2 Kings 19:9; Isaiah 37:9	7th century BC	Statues and Sphinx of Tirhakah Esarhaddon documents
King Uzziah (Azariah)	2 Kings 15:13-34; 2 Chronicles 26; 27; Isaiah 6:1	8th century BC	Uzziah burial plaque Stamp seal (bulla)
Yahweh	Numbers 6:24-26	9th–6th century BC	House of God Ostracon Ketef Hinnom amulets Mesha Stele

NEW TESTAMENT PERSONS CITED IN ANCIENT NON-CHRISTIAN SOURCES

PERSON	SCRIPTURES	SOURCES
Herod Agrippa I and II	Acts 12; 23:35; 25:13-26; 26	Philo, Josephus Coin inscriptions Nabatean Inscription Beirut Museum inscription
Ananias (High Priest)	Acts 23:2; 24:1	Josephus
Annas (High Priest)	Luke 3:2; Acts 4:6; John 18:13, 24	Josephus
Herod Antipas	Matthew 14:1-6; Mark 6:14-22; Luke 3:1; Acts 4:27; 13:1	Josephus Coin inscriptions that read "Herod the Tetrarch"
Herod Archelaus	Matthew 2:22	Josephus
King Aretas IV (Damascus)	2 Corinthians 11:32	Josephus Madaba Map inscription Coins with Aretas's bust
Caesar Augustus (Octavius)	Luke 2:2	Priene inscription announcing birthday Coin inscriptions Funerary inscription (*Res Gestae Divi Augusti*)
Bernice	Acts 25:13-15	Josephus Suetonius Beirut Museum inscription
Caiaphas (High Priest)		Josephus Ossuary inscription
Emperor Claudius	Acts 11:28; 18:2	Josephus Suetonius Tacitus Coin inscriptions
Drusilla	Acts 24:24	Josephus Suetonius
Erastus	Romans 16:13-23; 2 Timothy 4:20	Erastus inscription at Corinth
Marcus Antonius Felix	Acts 23:24-26; 24; 25:14; 26	Josephus Suetonius Tacitus
Porcius Festus	Acts 24:27; 25; 26:24, 32	Josephus
Gallio	Acts 18:12-17	Gallio inscription at Delphi Pliny the Younger Suetonius

PERSON	SCRIPTURES	SOURCES
Gamaliel	Acts 5:34; 22:3	Josephus Jewish Mishna Talmud
King Herod (Judea)	Matthew 2:1-22; Luke 1:5	Josephus Tacitus Coin inscriptions Herod's tomb at Herodium Latin wine jug inscription Herodian architecture (i.e., Temple Mount, Masada, Macherus, Herodium, etc.)
Herodias	Matthew 14:3; Mark 6:17	Josephus
James (Son of Mary)	Acts 15; James	James ossuary
James (Son of Zebedee)	Matthew 4:21; 10:2; Mark 5:37	Josephus
Jesus (of Nazareth)	Gospels	Josephus Tacitus Sutonius Pliny the Younger Lucian Babylonian Talmud Mara Bar Serapion Teledoth Jesu James ossuary inscription Megiddo mosaic floor inscription Alexamenos Graffito (picture)
John the Baptist	Matthew 3:1-13; Luke 1:7-39	Josephus Baptismal site (and steps) in Jordan at Jordan River John the Baptist cave (in progress)
Joseph (Adoptive Father of Jesus)	Matthew 1:20	James ossuary
Judas the Galilean	Acts 5:37	Josephus
Lysanias	Luke 3:1	Josephus Stone inscription at Abila (northern Morocco)
Herod Philip I (of Iturea)	Luke 3:1	Josephus
Herod Philip II (of Galilee)	Matthew 14:3; Mark 6:17; Luke 3:19	Josephus Coin inscriptions

PERSON	SCRIPTURES	SOURCES
Pontius Pilate	Luke 23:7, 22; John 18:31	Josephus Tacitus Philo Coins minted during his reign Pilate dedication stone inscription
Quirinius (Publius Sulpicius)	Luke 2:2	Josephus Tacitus Res Gestae inscription at Antioch Pisidia
Salome ("Daughter of Herodias")	Matthew 14:6	Josephus
Sergius Paulus	Acts 13:7	Two stone inscriptions (Cyprus and Rome) L. Sergius Paulus inscription (Pisidian Antioch, Turkey)
Theudas	Acts 5:36	Josephus
Caesar Tiberius	Luke 3:1	Josephus Tacitus Suetonius Marcus Velleius Paterculus Coin inscriptions Mentioned on Pilate dedication stone (Caesarea)

© Joseph M. Holden, 2013, 2020, adapted from Joseph M. Holden and Norman L. Geisler, *The Popular Handbook of Archaeology and the Bible: Discoveries That Confirm the Reliability of the Scripture* (Eugene, OR: Harvest House, 2013), 303–305.

NOTABLE
NEW TESTAMENT DISCOVERIES

ALEXAMENOS GRAFFITO

CAIAPHAS OSSUARY

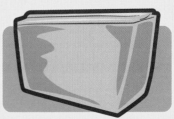

JAMES OSSUARY

PONTIUS PILATE INSCRIPTION

A CHRONOLOGY OF THE LIFE AND MINISTRY OF CHRIST

5–4 BC Jesus is born during the reigns of Herod the Great and Caesar Augustus (Matthew 2:1)

3 BC Jesus and family flee to Egypt due to persecution (Matthew 2:13-15)

AD 7–8 Jesus interacting with leaders at the temple at 12 years old (Luke 2:41-52)

AD 26 Jesus is baptized by John the Baptist (John 1:29-39)

Jesus is led into the wilderness and tempted by Satan (Matthew 4:1-11)

Christ begins ministry at about 30 years old (Luke 3:23)

Jesus performs his first miracle, turning water into wine at Cana (John 2:1-11)

AD 27 Christ's first Passover (John 2:13)

Jesus speaks with Nicodemus (John 3:1-21)

Jesus converses with the Samaritan woman (John 4:5-42)

Jesus heals the nobleman's son (John 4:46-54)

Peter, Andrew, James, and John follow Jesus (Matthew 4:18-22)

Matthew follows Jesus (Mark 2:13-17)

AD 28 Jesus chooses the 12 disciples (Mark 3:13-19)

Jesus teaches the Sermon on the Mount (Matthew 5–7)

Jesus calms the storm on the Sea of Galilee (Mark 4:35-41)

Jesus raises Jairus's daughter from the dead (Matthew 9:18-26)

Jesus sends the disciples out to spread the gospel (Matthew 9:35–11:1)

Herod imprisons John the Baptist at his palace at Machaerus (Jordan) (Matthew 14:1-12)

Christ's second Passover (John 5:1)

Herod kills John the Baptist (Matthew 14:1-12; Mark 6:14-29)

AD 29 Jesus feeds 5,000 (John 6:1-14)

Jesus walks on water at the Sea of Galilee (Mark 6:45-52)

Christ's third Passover (John 6:4)

Jesus feeds 4,000 (Matthew 15:32-39)

Peter confesses that Jesus is the Son of God (Matthew 16:13-20)

Jesus prepares his disciples for his death (Luke 9:22-25)

Jesus is transfigured on the mountain before Peter, James, and John (Matthew 17:1-13)

Jesus heals the man born blind (John 9:1-41)

Jesus raises Lazarus from the dead (John 11:1-44)

AD 30 Jesus speaks to the rich young ruler (Mark 10:17-31)

Jesus informs the disciples about his coming death and resurrection (Luke 18:31-34)

Jesus heals Bartimaeus (Luke 18:35-43)

Jesus visits Mary and Martha on his way to Jerusalem (John 11:55–12:1)

Mary Magdalene anoints Jesus (Matthew 26:6-13)

AD 30 (final week, Palm Sunday) Jesus rides into Jerusalem on a donkey (Matthew 21:1-17)

Jesus cleanses the temple (Mark 11:15-18)

The Jews scheme to betray Jesus (Luke 22:3-6)

Jesus eats his fourth Passover meal with the disciples Thursday evening (John 13:1-30)

Jesus gives the upper room discourse to his disciples (John 14–16)

Satan enters Judas, who betrays Jesus for 30 pieces of silver (John 13:21-30)

Jesus goes to the garden of Gethsemane with his disciples to pray (Matthew 26:30-46)

Judas arrives with the temple guards, who arrest Jesus in the garden (John 18:2-27)

Peter slices off Malchus's (servant of the high priest) ear (John 18:10-11)

Jesus rebukes Peter and restores Malchus's ear (Luke 22:48-51)

Jesus is arrested and placed on trial by the Sanhedrin (Luke 22:47-71)

Peter denies Jesus three times (John 18:15-27)

Jesus endures six trials and interrogation throughout the night and early morning hours (Matthew 27:2-26; John 18:2-27)

Jesus is tried and scourged by Pontius Pilate (John 19:1-3)

Jesus is sentenced to death by crucifixion (John 19:12-16)

Jesus is crucified on Friday with two criminals (Matthew 27:31-56; Luke 23:26-49)

Jesus gives charge of his mother, Mary, to John (John 19:25-27)

Jesus dies and is quickly buried in the tomb of Joseph of Arimathea due to the approaching Sabbath (Matthew 27:57-66; John 19:31-42)

Jesus remains in the tomb for three days (John 19:38–20:1)

Mary Magdalene discovers the tomb is empty (John 20:1-2)

Peter and John run to the tomb and find it empty (John 20:2-10)

Mary Magdalene sees the resurrected Jesus in the garden and tells the disciples (John 20:1-18)

AD 30 (post resurrection) Jesus shows himself for 40 days by many convincing proofs (Acts 1:3)

Jesus converses with the two men on the road to Emmaus (Luke 24:13-35)

Jesus appears multiple times and speaks to his disciples (John 20:19-25, 26-31; 21:1-25)

Jesus appears to skeptical Thomas (John 20:24-29)

Jesus has a breakfast meeting on the shores of Sea of Galilee with seven of the disciples, including Peter and John (John 21:1-25)

Jesus ascends to the Father in heaven (Matthew 28:16-20; Luke 24:44-53; Acts 1:9-11)

The day of Pentecost and the Holy Spirit arrive 50 days after Passover, and 10 days after the ascension to birth the church (Acts 1:4-5; 2:1-13)

THE MIRACLES OF JESUS

MIRACLE	LOCATION	TYPE	SCRIPTURE
Converts water to wine	Cana	Nature	John 2:1-11
Multiplies loaves and fish, feeds 5,000	Galilee	Nature	Matthew 14:15-21
Calms a storm	Sea of Galilee	Nature	Mark 4:35-41
Walks on water	Sea of Galilee	Nature	Matthew 14:22-33
Coin in the fish's mouth	Capernaum	Nature	Matthew 17:24-27
Feeds 4,000 people	Galilee	Nature	Matthew 15:32-39
Causes fig tree to wither	Journey to Jerusalem	Nature	Mark 11:12-25
Early large catch of fish	Sea of Galilee	Nature	Luke 5:1-11
Late large catch of fish	Sea of Galilee	Nature	John 21:1-14
Heals nobleman's son	Cana	Healing	John 4:46-54
Heals blind person	Bethsaida	Healing	Mark 8:22-26
Heals man born blind	Jerusalem	Healing	John 9:1-41
Raises Lazarus from the dead	Bethany	Healing	John 11:1-45
Casts out demon	Gadara (Galilee)	Healing	Mark 5:1-20
Raises Jairus's daughter from the dead	Capernaum	Healing	Matthew 9:18-26
Heals a crippled man at the pool of Bethesda	Jerusalem	Healing	John 5:1-18
Cures a bleeding woman	Capernaum	Healing	Luke 8:43-48
Heals a paralyzed man	Capernaum	Healing	Mark 2:1-12
Heals a leper	Galilee	Healing	Matthew 8:1-4
Restores health of Peter's mother-in-law	Capernaum	Healing	Matthew 8:14-17
Heals withered hand	Galilee	Healing	Matthew 12:9-14
Casts out demon from boy	Unknown	Healing	Mark 9:14-29
Heals demoniac and restores sight and speech	Galilee	Healing	Matthew 12:22
Restores sight to the blind men	Capernaum	Healing	Matthew 9:27-31
Heals demoniac and restores speech	Capernaum	Healing	Matthew 9:32-34
Heals hearing and speech	Southeast of Sea of Galilee (Jordan)	Healing	Mark 7:31-37
Restores Bartimaeus's sight	Jericho	Healing	Luke 18:35-43
Heals Syrophoenician girl	Tyre	Healing	Matthew 15:21-28
Heals centurion's servant	Capernaum	Healing	Luke 7:1-10
Heals demon-possessed man	Capernaum	Healing	Mark 1:23-27
Raises woman's son from the dead	Nain	Healing	Luke 7:11-16
Heals crippled woman	At a house, location unknown	Healing	Luke 13:10-17
Heals a man with dropsy	Jerusalem	Healing	Luke 14:1-6
Heals ten lepers	On a road, location unknown	Healing	Luke 17:11-19
Restores Malchus's ear	Jerusalem/garden of Gethsemane	Healing	John 18:10-11
Rises from the dead	Jerusalem tomb	Healing	John 20

MESSIANIC PROPHECIES OF CHRIST'S FIRST COMING AND FULFILLMENT

PROPHECY	SCRIPTURE	FULFILLMENT
Seed of the woman	Genesis 3:15	Galatians 4:4
Seed of Abraham	Genesis 12:2-3	Matthew 1:1
Seed of Isaac	Genesis 17:19	Matthew 1:2
Seed of Jacob	Numbers 24:17	Matthew 1:2
Seed of David	2 Samuel 7:12; Psalm 110:1; Micah 5:2	Matthew 22:43-44; Mark 12:36; John 7:42
From the tribe of Judah	Genesis 49:10	Luke 3:33
Would be incarnated as a man	Psalm 40:6-8	Philippians 2:1-11; Hebrews 10:5-9
Born in Bethlehem	Micah 5:2	Matthew 2:1-6
Born of a virgin	Isaiah 7:14	Matthew 1:22-23
The child that would be born	Isaiah 9:6	Luke 2:11
Specific time of birth	Daniel 9:25	Luke 2:1-2
Specific time of death	Daniel 9:26	John 19
Slaughter of babies	Jeremiah 31:15	Matthew 2:17-18
Right to the throne of David	Isaiah 9:7	Luke 1:32-33
Called out of Egypt	Hosea 11:1	Matthew 2:15
Ministry to Galilee region	Isaiah 9:1-2	Matthew 4:13-17
Prophet to come	Deuteronomy 18:15	Acts 3:20-22
Priest of the order of Melchizedek	Psalm 110:4	Hebrews 5:5-6
Came to heal hearts	Isaiah 61:1-2	Luke 4:18-19
Would have a healing ministry	Isaiah 53:4	Matthew 8:17
Would speak in parables	Psalm 78:2	Matthew 13:31-35
Someone would prepare the way for Messiah	Isaiah 40:3; Malachi 3:1; 4:5	Matthew 3:3; Mark 1:2-4; Luke 7:24-27
Messiah commissioned	Isaiah 6:1-2	Luke 4:18-21
Would be the Son of God	Psalm 2:7	Matthew 3:16-17
Would be God's Servant	Isaiah 42:1-4	Matthew 12:17-21; Philippians 2:7
Triumphal entry into Jerusalem	Zechariah 9:9	Mark 11:7-9
Would harden hearts	Isaiah 6:9-10; Isaiah 53:1	Matthew 13:14-15; Mark 4:12; Luke 8:10
Would have an unfaithful apostle	Psalm 109:8	John 17:12; Acts 1:20
Conspiracy against him	Psalm 2:1-2	Acts 4:25-27
The chief cornerstone	Psalm 118:22-23	Matthew 21:42; Mark 12:10
The stone of stumbling and an offense	Isaiah 8:14-15	Matthew 21: 42-44; Romans 9:32-33; 1 Peter 2:6-8
Would be betrayed	Psalm 41:9	Matthew 26:14-50
Betrayed for 30 pieces of silver	Zechariah 11:12	Matthew 26:15
Would be arrested	Zechariah 13:7	Matthew 26:54-56; Mark 14:48-49

PROPHECY	SCRIPTURE	FULFILLMENT
Disciples would leave him	Zechariah 13:7	Matthew 26:31, 56
Tried and condemned	Isaiah 53:8	Mark 15:1-15
False witnesses used to condemn him	Psalm 35:11	Matthew 26:59
Silent before his accusers	Isaiah 53:7	Matthew 27:12-14
Would be hated	Psalm 35:19	John 15:24-25
Rejected by his own people (Jews)	Isaiah 53:3	John 1:11
Would be spat upon and smitten	Isaiah 50:6	Matthew 26:67
Carried our sorrows and grief	Isaiah 53:4-5	Matthew 8:17; Romans 5:6-8
Would be sinless and without defect	Isaiah 53:9	1 Peter 2:22
Would be a vicarious sacrifice	Isaiah 53:5	Romans 5:6-8
Would be put to death as a criminal	Isaiah 53:12	Mark 15:27-28
Pierced through his hands and feet	Zechariah 12:10	John 20:27
Would be lifted up like the bronze serpent	Numbers 21:8-9	John 3:14-15
Would die	Deuteronomy 21:23; Isaiah 53:7-9	Acts 8:32-35; 1 Corinthians 15:3; Galatians 3:13
Reviled, scorned, and mocked while hanging on a tree	Psalm 22:7-8	Matthew 27:39, 43; Luke 23:35
Would thirst on the cross	Psalm 22:15	John 19:28
Given gall and vinegar	Psalm 69:21	Matthew 27:34
Prayed for his accusers	Psalm 109:2-5	Luke 23:34
Lots cast for his garments	Psalm 22:17-18	Matthew 27:35-36
Bones would not be broken	Psalm 34:20	John 19:32-36
Would be pierced	Zechariah 12:10	John 19:34
Would feel forsaken by God	Psalm 22:1	Matthew 27:46
Buried with the rich	Isaiah 53:9	Matthew 27:57-60
Would be resurrected	Psalm 16:8-11; 49:15	Mark 16:6-7
Death announced to bring in righteousness	Daniel 9:24	Matthew 27:46
Would ascend to the Father's right hand	Psalm 68:18; 110:1	Mark 16:19; Acts 1:6-11; Ephesians 4:8
Would view followers as brothers	Psalm 22:22; Isaiah 8:17-18	Hebrews 2:12-13

SELECT OLD TESTAMENT PROPHECIES ON CHRIST'S SECOND COMING

SCRIPTURE	DESCRIPTION
Psalm 50:2-5	Christ will come to judge and gather his people
Isaiah 9:6-7	Of his government and peace there will be no end
Isaiah 66:18	Christ will gather all the nations, and they will see his glory
Daniel 2:44	Christ will return and establish his kingdom after bringing an end to the revived Roman Empire
Daniel 7:13-14	Christ will come with the clouds of heaven, and his kingdom will last forever
Zechariah 12:9-10	Christ will destroy his enemies and present himself to the people of Israel as the one whom they pierced
Zechariah 14:4-9	Christ will return to the Mount of Olives and set up his earthly kingdom

SELECT NEW TESTAMENT SCRIPTURES ABOUT CHRIST'S SECOND COMING

MATTHEW 16:27: "The Son of Man is going to come with his angels in the glory of his Father, and then he will repay each person according to what he has done."

MATTHEW 24:27: "As the lightning comes from the east and shines as far as the west, so will be the coming of the Son of Man."

MATTHEW 24:29: "Immediately after the tribulation of those days the sun will be darkened, and the moon will not give its light, and the stars will fall from heaven, and the powers of the heavens will be shaken."

MATTHEW 24:30-31: "Then will appear in heaven the sign of the Son of Man, and then all the tribes of the earth will mourn, and they will see the Son of Man coming on the clouds of heaven with power and great glory. And he will send out his angels with a loud trumpet call, and they will gather his elect from the four winds, from one end of heaven to the other."

MATTHEW 24:36: "Concerning that day and hour no one knows, not even the angels of heaven, nor the Son, but the Father only."

MATTHEW 24:37-39: "As were the days of Noah, so will be the coming of the Son of Man. For as in those days before the flood they were eating and drinking, marrying and giving in marriage, until the day when Noah entered the ark, and they were unaware until the flood came and swept them all away, so will be the coming of the Son of Man."

MATTHEW 24:42: "Stay awake, for you do not know on what day your Lord is coming."

MATTHEW 24:43-44: "Know this, that if the master of the house had known in what part of the night the thief was coming, he would have stayed awake and would not have let his house be broken into. Therefore you also must be ready, for the Son of Man is coming at an hour you do not expect."

MATTHEW 25:31: "When the Son of Man comes in his glory, and all the angels with him, then he will sit on his glorious throne."

MARK 8:38: "Whoever is ashamed of me and of my words in this adulterous and sinful generation, of him will the Son of Man also be ashamed when he comes in the glory of his Father with the holy angels."

MARK 9:1: "He said to them, 'Truly, I say to you, there are some standing here who will not taste death until they see the kingdom of God after it has come with power.'"

LUKE 21:34-36: "Watch yourselves lest your hearts be weighed down with dissipation and drunkenness and cares of this life, and that day come upon you suddenly like a trap. For it will come upon all who dwell on the face of the whole earth. But stay awake at all times, praying that you may have strength to escape all these things that are going to take place, and to stand before the Son of Man."

JOHN 14:1-3: "Let not your hearts be troubled. Believe in God; believe also in me. In my Father's house are many rooms. If it were not so, would I have told you that I go to prepare a place for you? And if I go and prepare a place for you, I will come again and will take you to myself, that where I am you may be also."

ACTS 1:9-11: "When he had said these things, as they were looking on, he was lifted up, and a cloud took him out of their sight. And while they were gazing into heaven as he went, behold, two men stood by them in white robes, and said, 'Men of Galilee, why do you stand looking into heaven? This Jesus, who was taken up from you into heaven, will come in the same way as you saw him go into heaven.'"

ACTS 3:19-21: "Repent therefore, and turn back, that your sins may be blotted out, that times of refreshing may come from the presence of the Lord, and that he may send the Christ appointed for you, Jesus, whom heaven must receive until the time for restoring all the things about which God spoke by the mouth of his holy prophets long ago."

1 CORINTHIANS 4:5: "Do not pronounce judgment before the time, before the Lord comes, who will bring to light the things now hidden in darkness and will disclose the purposes of the heart. Then each one will receive his commendation from God."

1 THESSALONIANS 5:2: "You yourselves are fully aware that the day of the Lord will come like a thief in the night."

2 THESSALONIANS 2:8: "Then the lawless one will be revealed, whom the Lord Jesus will kill with the breath of his mouth and bring to nothing by the appearance of his coming."

TITUS 2:13: "...waiting for our blessed hope, the appearing of the glory of our great God and Savior Jesus Christ."

HEBREWS 9:28: "Christ, having been offered once to bear the sins of many, will appear a second time, not to deal with sin but to save those who are eagerly waiting for him."

HEBREWS 10:24-25: "Let us consider how to stir up one another to love and good works, not neglecting to meet together, as is the habit of some, but encouraging one another, and all the more as you see the Day drawing near."

1 PETER 1:13: "Preparing your minds for action, and being sober-minded, set your hope fully on the grace that will be brought to you at the revelation of Jesus Christ."

2 PETER 3:10: "The day of the Lord will come like a thief, and then the heavens will pass away with a roar, and the heavenly bodies will be burned up and dissolved, and the earth and the works that are done on it will be exposed."

1 JOHN 3:2-3: "Beloved, we are God's children now, and what we will be has not yet appeared; but we know that when he appears we shall be like him, because we shall see him as he is. And everyone who thus hopes in him purifies himself as he is pure."

REVELATION 1:7-8: "Behold, he is coming with the clouds, and every eye will see him, even those who pierced him, and all tribes of the earth will wail on account of him. Even so. Amen. 'I am the Alpha and the Omega,' says the Lord God, 'who is and who was and who is to come, the Almighty.'"

REVELATION 16:15: "Behold, I am coming like a thief! Blessed is the one who stays awake, keeping his garments on, that he may not go about naked and be seen exposed!"

REVELATION 17:14: "They will make war on the Lamb, and the Lamb will conquer them, for he is Lord of lords and King of kings, and those with him are called and chosen and faithful."

REVELATION 19:11-21: "I saw heaven opened, and behold, a white horse! The one sitting on it is called Faithful and True, and in righteousness he judges and makes war. His eyes are like a flame of fire, and on his head are many diadems, and he has a name written that no one knows but himself. He is clothed in a robe dipped in blood, and the name by which he is called is The Word of God. And the armies of heaven, arrayed in fine linen, white and pure, were following him on white horses. From his mouth comes a sharp sword with which to strike down the nations, and he will rule them with a rod of iron. He will tread the winepress of the fury of the wrath of God the Almighty. On his robe and on is thigh he has a name written, King of kings and Lord of lords...And I saw the beast and the kings of the earth with their armies gathered to make war against him who was sitting on the horse and against his army. And the best was captured, and with it the false prophet who in its presence had done the signs by which he deceived those who had received the mark of the beast and those who worshiped its image. These two were thrown into the lake of fire that burns with sulfur. And the rest were slain by the sword that came from the mouth of him who was sitting on the horse, and all the birds were gorged with their flesh."

REVELATION 22:12: "Behold, I am coming soon, bringing my recompense with me, to repay everyone for what he has done."

REVELATION 22:20: "He who testifies to these things says, 'Surely I am coming soon.' Amen. Come, Lord Jesus!"

WHAT WE KNOW ABOUT HELL

Hell is where unbelievers will be eternally separated from God in accord with their own free will. The torment of hell appears to be characterized by three conditions: (1) privation, (2) pain, and (3) punishment.

Torment vs. Torture

Some have mistakenly equated the biblical word *torment* with notions of *torture*. There is a big difference between the two: *Torture* refers to the infliction of pain from without against one's will, and *torment* is the infliction of pain that originates from within in accordance with one's will. Torment emerges from regret over a life of unforgiven sin.

Necessity of HELL

God honors every person's decision about Christ. He will not force anyone to love him or dwell with him forever in heaven. Forced love is contradictory. Therefore, God has provided a place for those who choose to reject Christ, and it is here that they will be punished for unforgiven sin. There are several reasons hell is necessary:

1 God's love makes hell necessary; he will not violate anyone's will. God loves people so much that he will ensure their preferences are fulfilled.

2 Equity makes hell necessary, for not all evils are punished in this life.

3 Victory over evil makes hell necessary because victory requires an eternal quarantine that separates good from evil. The presence of hell ensures that evil will not interrupt good, and good will not interrupt evil.

4 Hell must be eternal because people have sinned against an eternal God—they must be given an eternal punishment for an eternal crime. In addition, the quarantine of hell must last as long as heaven does. The same Greek word translated "eternal" (*aionion*) is used to describe eternal condemnation and eternal life.

5 God's love for people is such that he will not annihilate the wicked. For him to do so would mean attacking his own image, in which people are created (Genesis 1:26-27; 9:6).

6 Christ's agony and death on the cross would be meaningless if hell was not a real place to be avoided.

7 Hell was originally prepared for the devil and his fallen angels (demons) to punish them for rebelling against God (Matthew 25:41).

KEY WORDS RELATING TO THE AFTERLIFE:

Sheol—A Hebrew word that can be used to refer to the grave, hell, a pit, or the abode of the dead.

Hades—A Greek word that can be used to refer to a place of departed souls, the grave, or a place of torment.

Gehenna—A Greek term that refers to a place or state of everlasting punishment.

Tartaros—A Greek term that refers to confinement, incarceration, or a place of eternal torment.

HOW TO AVOID HELL

AND GO TO HEAVEN

RECOGNIZE

that you are a sinner who has fallen short of the glory of God (Romans 3:23).

REALIZE

that God loves you so much he sent his Son to die on the cross to pay the penalty for your sins—a debt you couldn't possibly pay (Romans 5:6-8).

REPENT

of your sin to and ask God to forgive you (Romans 3:24-26; 1 John 1:9).

EXERCISE

faith in Christ as your personal Savior and receive the gift of eternal life—salvation is a gift and cannot be earned through good works (Romans 6:23; 10:9-10).

WHAT WE KNOW ABOUT HEAVEN

WHAT IS HEAVEN LIKE?

- It has many rooms and dwellings (John 14:2; 2 Corinthians 5:1)
- It is where God will dwell with us on his throne (Psalm 11:4; Isaiah 66:1; Revelation 21:3)
- It is where we will go when we die to be with the Lord (2 Corinthians 5:8)
- It is where we will be together with Christ (John 14:3)
- It is called the "third heaven" (2 Corinthians 12:2)
- It is called "paradise" (Luke 23:43; 2 Corinthians 12:3; Revelation 2:7)
- Great things are uttered there that cannot be repeated in this life (2 Corinthians 12:4)
- It is a place of comfort and security (Luke 16:25)
- It is a place of rewards (Matthew 5:12)
- It is a place of joy (Luke 15:7)
- It is a place of music and victory (Revelation 15:2)
- It is a place of life and vitality (Revelation 22:1-3)
- It is illuminated by God's glory (Revelation 21:23)
- It is where the New Jerusalem will be located (Revelation 21:16)
- We will worship God and the Lamb (Revelation 22:3)
- We will see the Lamb's face and his name will be on our foreheads (Revelation 22:4)
- We will reign forever and ever with God and the Lamb (Revelation 22:5)

WHAT WILL NOT BE IN HEAVEN

- The first heaven and first earth will pass away (Revelation 21:1)
- There will be no marriage (Matthew 22:29-30)
- There will be no sea (Revelation 21:1)
- There will be no sin (Revelation 21:27)
- There will be no pain (Revelation 21:4)
- There will be no curse (Revelation 22:3)
- There will be no separation from God (Revelation 21:4)
- There will be no sorrow (Revelation 21:4)
- There will be no night nor darkness (Revelation 21:5)
- There will be no crying (Revelation 21:4)
- There will be no mourning (Revelation 21:4)
- There will be no death (Revelation 21:4)
- There will be no faithless and detestable individuals (Revelation 21:8)
- There will be nothing unclean (Revelation 21:27)
- There will be no hunger or heat exhaustion (Revelation 7:16-17)
- There will be no need of the sun or the moon for light (Revelation 21:23)
- There will be no temple, for the temple is God Almighty and the Lamb (Revelation 21:22)

To learn more about Harvest House books and
to read sample chapters, visit our website:

www.harvesthousepublishers.com

HARVEST HOUSE PUBLISHERS
EUGENE, OREGON